THE
UNICORN
IN THE
SANCTUARY

The New Age Movement
in the Catholic Church

Randy England

TRINITY COMMUNICATIONS
MANASSAS, VA 22110

TO MY WIFE

ISBN 0-937495-36-0

Table of Contents

THE UNICORN

One of the most common symbols that new
agers use as an identifying device is the unicorn.
The unicorn is a symbol of New Age transformation:
a symbol of destruction and renewal. This
mythical animal has often been associated
in literature with both Christ (wrongly)
and with Lucifer. It is not the cute
and gentle creature popularly
portrayed . . . but a symbol
of tearing and trampling,
breaking and crushing.

Permission for material from *Sadhana: A Way to God, Christian
Exercises in Eastern Form* by Anthony De Mello (sixth printing,
1984) granted by Institute of Jesuit Sources, St. Louis, MO.

Foreword

When C. S. Lewis wrote of the distasteful task of writing his popular book *The Screwtape Letters*, he described the job of getting inside the devil's head "as all dust, grit, thirst, and itch. It almost smothered me before I was done." Any survey of the New Age movement is likewise "dust, grit, thirst, and itch" but with a difference: the corruption is masked by a welcoming veneer. The material is at once revolting and enticing; blasphemous and seductive. To live is to know sorrow. Intolerable poverty and starvation, cruelty, murder and war are widespread now, as always. This sick world screams for an answer, a leader, a solution to its predicament. "For we know that all creation groans and travails in pain until now." (Romans 8:22). The New Age movement promises hope for peace. Hope for a better life. It appeals to man's sensuality, for in the New Age movement there is no sin as we know it; and more important: no guilt. Finally, and even more energizing than appeals to sensuality, the New Age movement entices the proud with promises of power and of godhood.

The New Age Movement holds out all these things, but at a price; a price that Jesus warns us is no bargain: "For what does profit a man if he gain the whole world, but suffer loss of his own soul? Or what will a man give in exchange for his soul?" (Matthew 16:26).

A half dozen years ago few had even heard of the New Age movement. Now nearly everyone has. Other related movements or labels are: Human Potential Movement, Modernism, New Thought, Globalism, and the Aquarian Conspiracy. Parts of it include Mind Control Classes, the Holistic Health Movement, Transcendental Meditation, Humanistic Psychology, Positive Confession, Feminist Spirituality, Positive Mental Attitude, the New Physics, and numerous political organizations, as well as other esoteric, environmental and animal rights groups.

I had heard of many of these before, but in 1983 I first learned from a radio program how they were tied together into a single whole. Author Constance Cumbey, who has since produced two books on the New Age Movement, was speaking about her research on the movement. The story was, to me, incredible but at the same time seemed to fit the facts. Soon after, I found the book *Peace, Prosperity and the Coming Holocaust* by cult expert Dave Hunt and read it through the same night. In finishing, I was both electrified and skeptical. It was all too big, too encompassing and too unbelievable, so I resolved to be vigilant as to its influence but to avoid the awkwardness of sharing with anyone else that which I had barely begun to believe myself. My resolve lasted not twenty four hours.

The next evening I sat down to dinner with a friend and soon found myself regurgitating all that I had read. I told him about how occult teachings had been incorporated into the fabric of our institutions; into politics, into the churches, into business and sports. I told him about courses that teach people how to control their minds so as to control every aspect of their lives; how these teachings were strikingly similar to Nazism; how they are anti-semitic, anti-God and anti-Christian. I told him how most of the writings of the movement had been produced through automatic writing by which spirits allegedly speak through the authors. I even explained that many New Agers actually had spirit guides with whom they had frequent contact while in altered states of consciousness and that these "guides" ruled their lives.

My friend became quieter as I talked on for at least an hour. Finally becoming convinced that he thought me mad, I stopped and waited for some response. He had asked no questions and now looked at me grimly.

He said, "You haven't told me anything I don't already know." I restrained my surprise as I waited for him to go on.

"Last week," he started, "my mother filed for divorce from my father. She belongs to a group connected with our church. Each person in the group has two spirit guides which come to them while they meditate. The guides supposedly give you advice and help you with problems. One of my mother's guides is Jesus. Her guides had been wanting her to get my father involved with the group but he is not interested, so they ordered Mom to leave him. That's how I know about the New Age Movement."

From that point on, I began to research the Movement and quickly found that many individuals in my own church had deep involvement, both in the present and in the past. In showing the avenues that the Movement has paved into the Church, I have tried to follow the evidence wherever it would lead. If the reader finds a personal hero or two entangled in New Age concepts it should not necessarily be taken as an indictment of those individuals. Rather, it is an indication of how far this influence has spread and has been taken into the life of the Church. I can only hope that Truth has not been sustained at the expense of Charity.

In attempting to discern errors, one runs—of course—the risk of finding them, and in finding and exposing them one commits the supreme "sin" of intolerance. Western culture, which can seemingly stomach any perversity, is quite intolerant about one thing: intolerance. We live in a society that values, perhaps above all, tolerance. Tolerance of other viewpoints, especially religious viewpoints, is demanded.

The reason for such tolerance lies not with any truth inherent in divergent viewpoints. Such a notion would be absurd, as two contradictory beliefs cannot both be true. But tolerance is preferable to intolerance not because men are wise and good but because men are evil and cannot be trusted to deal justly with their fellow man. For this reason, a large measure of tolerance is a virtue in this world.

Within the Church, however, there must be limits beyond which the title "Christian" can no longer apply. The Church is not wedded to the passions of the moment, but bound to the truth without regard for any momentary twists currently popular with those individuals who are given over to the latest scientific or philosophic musings. This "dogmatic relativism" was rejected by Pius XII in the Encyclical *Humani Generis*. He wrote that the way in which we express the truth

> is capable of being perfected and polished; and we know also that the Church itself has not always used the same terms in the same way. [But] it is also manifest that the Church cannot be bound to every system of philosophy that has existed for a short space of time.
>
> This is supreme impudence and something that would make dogma itself a reed shaken by the wind.[1]

The Apostle Peter was neither sparing nor gentle in his condemnations. He warned the faithful:

> Among you there will be lying teachers who will bring in destructive sects. They will even disown the Lord who bought them, thus bringing upon themselves swift destruction.
>
> For it were better for them not to have known the way of justice, than having known it, to turn back on the holy commandment delivered to them. (2 Peter 2:1,21).

Scripture is clear in its treatment of those who steadfastly bring shame on the body of Christ. St. Paul brooks no compromise in his First Letter to the Corinthians:

> I wrote you in my letter not to associate with the immoral—not meaning, of course, the immoral of this world, or the covetous or the greedy, or idolators; otherwise you would have to leave the world! But now I write to you not to associate with one who is called a brother, if he is immoral,

---

[1]Pius XII, *Humani Generis* (Daughters of St. Paul, Boston, Massachusetts, 1950) 16-17.

or covetous, or an idolator, or evil-tongued, or a drunkard, or greedy; with such a one not even to take food. For what have I to do with judging those outside? Is it not those inside whom you must judge. For those outside God will judge. Expel the wicked man from your midst. (1 Corinthians 5:9-13)

This, then, is the basis of my "intolerance." Criticism is easy and I will, as much as possible, try to let individuals speak for themselves. The purpose is not to condemn the individuals involved but to permit the reader to understand these errors and the forces behind them. God knows fully what motives lay behind words and actions and He will judge correctly. Nevertheless, it is every Catholic's duty to judge teachings and actions in light of the truth he claims to hold and serve. This book, then, is an effort at sound judgment in the light of truth.

Randy England

Introduction:

Change . . . or Exchange?

*"They exchanged the truth of God for a lie,
and worshipped and served the creature
rather than the creator...."*
   (Romans 1:25)

What is happening in the Church today? Are the changes we have experienced in the more than twenty years since Vatican II nothing more than the Catholic Church's entry into the modern age? For myself, I could understand the transition to the use of the vernacular at Mass, but some people are still uncomfortable with it. Other changes, such as the liturgical use of different musical instruments (besides the organ), have been widely accepted. Still, many Catholics find the guitar mass distasteful. Unfortunately, those faithful who are not comfortable with change are subtly ridiculed as reactionaries or worse. But who has not been uncomfortable with certain of the following novelties?

Novelties such as:

- A separate "feminist spirituality" for women that goes "beyond God the Father" and instead celebrates self and seeks to connect with nature or "the Goddess." Such a system demands a

matriarchal society and cannot accept a male God
or Savior.

- A new "mission" for missionaries which does not
  include any motive of conversion. Missionaries
  who seek "wisdom" at the feet of Hindu holy men
  and whose writings quote from the Hindu and
  Chinese scriptures with more awe and reverence
  than they accord the Bible. Catholic priests who
  run Hindu ashrams disguised as Catholic "retreat
  houses" and Catholic bishops who support them.

- "New Age" Catholic schools that are chiefly interested in teaching values for a one world government and the coming new age. Such basic items as
  the Ten Commandments and belief in the resurrection are considered dispensable.

- A Jesuit from India who has taught Eastern
  meditation to Catholic clergy and laity alike. His
  techniques bring the "seeker" into contact with
  demons visualized as wise spirit guides.

- An extremely popular Dominican priest who
  maintains that the practice of traditional Christianity is equivalent to "whoring after past gods."
  In the New Age, we are to worship the creation...and the creature.

- Courses, tapes and books that promise to "teach
  us how to pray." These new prayers, billed as ancient Christian techniques, turn out to be doorways to altered states of consciousness and
  demonic realms.

- The rehabilitation of the condemned teachings of
  Jesuit Pierre Teilhard de Chardin. Teilhard is the
  premier inspiration for New Agers, both Catholic
  and non-Catholic alike.

- A Catholic theologian who accepts the possibility of reincarnation and that God will ultimately relent and allow all men into heaven. He expects that shamanism (witchcraft) will become the norm as we move into a New Age of global consciousness.

- A Franciscan priest who travels the circuit of Catholic churches and convents teaching the faithful how to manipulate reality with their minds using the aid and counsel of spirit beings.

- Numerous large national Catholic publishers who peddle books and tapes which include yoga, mantra chanting, New Age music, healing meditations, Eastern religions and Intensive Journaling through occult meditation. These are all presented as avenues to enhanced Catholic "spirituality."

These examples are of a completely different order than the external changes the church has experienced. Any question regarding missing communion rails or the "folk" mass pale in the face of such issues as the Deity of Jesus Christ and the Way of salvation.

Unfortunately change, even needed change, has long coattails. The often cited "Spirit of Vatican II" has too often been ample excuse for innovators to experiment with a faith which, for them, has lost its meaning. Their beliefs are generally part of what is known as the New Age movement. This book will show how its pagan philosophy has infiltrated the life and institutions of the Catholic Church.

St. John the Apostle, an old man exiled on the Aegean island of Patmos for proclaiming the word of God, received an appropriate message from Our Lord and addressed it to a church that had a fine reputation in the world. The message was simple: "Wake up, and strengthen what remains before it dies" (Revelation 3:2).

The Church has survived two thousand years, much of that time under attack. Yet, in the last one hundred years, the breeze has stiffened; there is a malignancy in the air—the breath of the evil one. True, man is capable of much mischief, but the New Age movement is not from men. It is from hostile, superintelligent beings masquerading as angels of light. Their appeal is to brother-hood and peace for a miserable world—a world ripe for harvest and judgment.

1.

The New Age Movement

"The soul goes round upon a wheel of stars and all
things return.... Good and evil go round in a wheel
that is one thing and not many. Do you not realize
in your heart, do you not believe behind all your
beliefs, that there is but one reality and we are its
shadows; and that all things are but aspects of one
thing; a center where men melt into Man and Man
into God?"

"No," said Father Brown.
   —G. K. Chesterton, *The Dagger with Wings*

Ideally, I would launch immediately into my subject, but the
matter requires a familiarity with the material and its history.
Readers already familiar with the background of the New Age
movement may wish to skim this chapter.

The New Age movement is a worldwide phenomenon ostensib-
ly dedicated to the ideas of the interconnectedness of all things and
the powers of the human mind. In the New Age, knowledge super-
sedes faith and heralds a break with western values and thought.
Its goals are a one world government, a one world religion, and a
one world Christ. These are not necessarily bad: not necessarily
unChristian. The question is which Christ? Which Religion?

Regarding a one world government, the Bible seems to show that a united mankind—not under God, but under man's own flag—is not a good thing. It has been tried before. At the Tower of Babel, God had to intervene in order to put down man's arrogant effort to set himself up as his own god. God knew the evil result and prevented our unification. Confusing the language and scattering mankind throughout the earth, God graciously kept us from our own pride. (Genesis 11:19). We need only to look around at how some nations now oppress and even murder their own citizens. At least they are restrained in part by the disapproval of other nations and in greater part by their own borders. What will the torturers do when they know neither borders nor disapproving onlookers? Apart from grace, fallen man cannot live as one. The fantasy must wait.

St. Paul writes unequivocally that a new world leader will appear before the second coming of Christ. The Apostle tells of a great falling away from the Church and the rise of the anti-Christ or "man of sin:"

> Let no one deceive you in any way, for the day of the Lord will not come unless the apostasy comes first, and the man of sin is revealed, the son of perdition, who opposes and is exalted above all that is called God, or that is worshipped, so that he sits in the temple of God and gives himself out as if he were God. And now you know what restrains him, that he may be revealed in his proper time. For the mystery of iniquity is already at work; provided only that he who is at present restraining it, does still restrain, until he is gotten out of the way. And the wicked one will be revealed, whom the Lord Jesus Christ will slay with the breath of his mouth and will destroy with the brightness of his coming. And his coming is according to the working of Satan with all power and signs and lying wonders, and with all wicked deception to those who are perishing. For they have not received the love of truth that they might be saved. Therefore God sends them a misleading influence that they may believe the falsehood, that all may be judged who have not

believed the truth, but have preferred wickedness. (II Thessalonians 2:3-12)

The *Didache* or "Teachings of the Twelve Apostles," which is one of the earliest extra-biblical Christian documents, taught: "For in the last days...the Deceiver of the world will appear, claiming to be the Son of God, and giving striking exhibitions of power; the earth will be given over to his hands...." (*Didache* 16:4).[1]

The "restrainer" referred to by St. Paul has variously been explained as St. Michael the Archangel, or the presence of the Church or the Holy Spirit. This "restrainer" of the anti-Christ may be removed directly by God or may reflect the removal of the influence of the Church or Holy Spirit as a result of the apostasy.

We wonder, as did Jesus' disciples: "When are these things to happen?" And Jesus tells us: "But of that day and hour no one knows, not even the angels of heaven, but the Father only." (Matthew 24:3, 36). What is certain is that the day will come, and when it does come it may be the New Age movement which fosters the apostasy; it may be the very delusion which will prepare the world for the anti-Christ.

The New Age movement is as old as mankind, and although its beliefs have probably never been without adherents, it needs no human continuity to maintain its ancient tenets, for all its essential elements flow straight from hell. The first victims of the New Age movement are well known. In fact, we have all inherited an attraction for its lies: And the woman answered him [the serpent] saying:

> "Of the fruit of the trees that are in the paradise we do eat; but of the fruit of the tree in the midst of paradise, God hath commanded us that we should not eat; and that we should not touch it, lest perhaps we die." And the serpent said to the woman: "No, you shall not die the death! For

---

[1]James A. Kleist, S.J., Ph.D.(translator), *Ancient Christian Writers: The Works of the Fathers in Translation* (Newman Press, Westminster, Maryland, 1948) pg. 24.

God knows that in what day you eat of it, your eyes shall be
opened and you shall be as gods, knowing good and evil."
(Genesis 3:2,3).

These two lies are the foundation of every pagan religion and
cult:

- You will not die.
- You will be like God.

In every imaginable fashion these ideas are woven into endless
patterns along with enough truth to fool nearly anyone. They are
found in the doctrines of reincarnation and the divinity of man. In
the New Age, the wages of sin is not death, but just another go
around in another life. Nothing really matters. There is no personal
Creator God to interfere with the attractions of pride and sensuality—no one to whom we must give account. And even if God
did exist, what claim could he make upon us, His fellow gods?

Modernism, Immanence and Pantheism

The modern equivalent of the New Age movement began to
exert a strong influence in the seminaries of the Church before the
turn of the century. Strangely enough, this old heresy was called by
the name of "modernism." Pope Pius X, in his encyclical *Pascendi
Gregis* or *On the Doctrines of the Modernists*, undertook a description
of the problem, realizing how obscure, shadowy and unconnected
all the threads seemed. Nevertheless, he boldly traced the connections and exposed Modernism, beginning a period of purification
that unfortunately died soon after him. From the encyclical, *Pascendi*:

> We must now interrupt a silence, which it would be
> criminal to prolong, that we may point out to the whole
> Church, as they really are, men who are badly disguised.
>   It is one of the cleverest devices of the Modernists...to
> present their doctrines without order and systematic arran-
> gement in a scattered and disjointed manner so as to make
> it appear as if their minds were in doubt or hesitation,

whereas in reality they are quite firm and steadfast. For this reason it will be of advantage to bring their teachings together here into one group, and to point out their interconnection....[2]

Christians have always worshipped the God who created the universe. He made it from nothing and is distinct from it. "For thou hast created all things, and because of thy will they existed and were created" (Revelation 4:11).

The doctrine of immanence is the idea that God is not separate and distinct from His creation but that He is (somehow) diffused throughout it while at the same time the creation is (somehow) diffused throughout God. And yet we have been taught (and the Church has always taught) a similar idea; that God is omnipresent. This is clear from scripture as King David wrote:

> Where can I go from your spirit? From your presence where can I flee?
> If I go up to the heavens you are there; If I sink to the nether world, you are present there.
> If I take the wings of the dawn, If I settle at the farthest limits of the sea.
> Even there your hand shall guide me, and your right hand hold me fast.   (Psalms 138:7-10)

Apart from this natural omnipresence, there is also the supernatural presence of God through His grace. Truly, every member of Christ's church is indwelt by the Holy Spirit, but neither is this what is meant by immanence.

Proponents of this sort of "immanence" believe either that there is no God out there at all or that if He is out there, then he is unknowable. In practice, this means that man must not look outward to a God separate from himself, but rather to the god

---

[2] Pope St. Pius X, *Pascendi Gregis* (Burns & Oates, Ltd., London, 1907) pg 56.

within. We must look inside ourselves if we will learn of God. In fact, the Modernist New Age perspective considers the concept of a God outside ourselves to be absurd and even revolting. The key is to go within. Pius X understood the distinction when he wrote: "Religion...must, like every other fact, admit of some explanation. [When] all external revelation [is] absolutely denied, it is clear that this explanation will be sought in vain outside of man himself. It must, therefore, be looked for in man."[3]

As Pius X produced his encyclical, G.K. Chesterton was writing his classic work, *Orthodoxy*. In it, he spoke of the insufficiency of the "Inner Light":

> Of all the conceivable forms of enlightenment the worst is what these people call the Inner Light. Of all horrible religions the most horrible is the worship of the god within. Any one who knows any body (sic) knows how it would work.... That Jones shall worship the god within him turns out ultimately to mean that Jones shall worship Jones. Let Jones worship the sun or moon, anything rather than the Inner Light; let Jones worship cats or crocodiles, if he can find any in his street, but not the god within. Christianity came into the world firstly in order to assert with violence, that a man had not only to look inwards, but to look outwards, to behold with astonishment and enthusiasm a divine company and a divine captain. The only fun of being a Christian was that a man was not left alone with the Inner Light, but definitely recognized an outer light, fair as the sun, clear as the moon, terrible as an army with banners.
>
> That transcendence and distinctness of the deity which some Christians now want to remove from Christianity,

---

[3]*Ibid.*, pg 8.

was really the only reason why anyone wanted to be a Christian.[4]

Pius X taught that the Modernists' (and I would add the New Agers') concept of "god immanent" squares best with Pantheism. He asked, "Does or does not this 'immanence' leave God distinct from man? If it does not, it is Pantheism."[5] Pantheism, simply means that God is Everything and that Everything is God. Pantheism is the natural upshot of the doctrine of immanence, though many Catholic New Agers (forgive the oxymoron) try to draw convoluted arguments to the contrary. One popular writer-speaker-Dominican priest has tried to sidestep the charge of heresy by calling the doctrine of God immanent "panentheism" or as he explains it: "God is in everything, and everything is in God."[6]

With just a little verbal shuffling, the lie is made palatable. The phrase may not be instantly recognized as false, but something is wrong. Often, the New Ager will use innocent sounding language but with a new and different twist. In this example the writer uses his "panentheism" as a starting point from which he develops what eventually turns out to be open paganism and witchcraft, but more on that later.

No matter what you call it, pantheism dilutes the idea of God so thoroughly that in the end all meaning disappears. In J.D Salinger's story, "Teddy" a ten year old boy recounts his realization of the pantheistic God: "I was six when I saw that everything was God.... It was on a Sunday, I remember. My sister was...drinking her milk and all of a sudden I saw that she was God and the milk

---

[4]G.K. Chesterton, *Orthodoxy* (Image Books, Garden City, NY, 1959) pp 76-78.

[5]Pius X, *Pascendi*, pg 23, 50.

[6]Matthew Fox, *Original Blessing* (Bear & Company, Santa Fe, NM, 1983) pg 90.

was God. I mean all she was doing was pouring God into God, if you know what I mean."[7]

Holism, Hinduism and Reincarnation

Holism is the view that all things are interconnected and form a single entity. This entity or "whole" has an independent reality which is greater than the sum of its parts. This is the viewpoint of Hinduism and has its foundation in the experience of the individual.

In Christianity, our leaders are those who, through their faith and obedience to God, teach us about Him. Some of our earliest teachers were directly inspired by God to write the Bible. The Hindu teacher, or guru, should not be seen in the same way, but rather as a tour guide.

It is as if, when John on Patmos had received the Revelation, rather than writing down the revealed truth, he opened a school instructing aspiring Christians in his methods for corresponding with God. He would insist that the truth was impossible to communicate. John's advice would be for the Christian to make his own connection with the source. That is the advice now popular with many Catholic teachers today.

It is the task of the guru to teach methods, not doctrine. The aim is to achieve an altered state of consciousness during which the seeker experiences the "oneness" of all things. In the West we see one thing as being distinct from another. If I say "This is a chair and this is a dog and this is my foot," anyone listening would understand. The Hindu or Buddhist would maintain that these things are not at all distinct from one another. Instead, it is I that have arbitrarily imposed my view of reality.

---

[7]J.D. Salinger, *Nine Stories* (Little, Brown and Company Boston, MA, 1953) pg 288.

More to the point, these particulars have no reality at all. They are illusion. The only reality is that of the mind; the only purpose: to achieve a oneness with the universal mind. We are to get past the logical view and "realize" that there is no separation between the self and all others. The guru's job is to show the way.

The fact that the individual must experience for himself this ultimate does not mean there is no actual doctrine. The "truths" experienced can be expressed in words, but cannot actually be "known" without the experience. This is not a religion of faith and reason, but of experiential knowledge. The belief system generated through altered states of consciousness is strikingly similar from one individual to the next. The distance between experiences may be a thousand miles or a thousand years, but the message is the same. This remarkable (but not perfect) agreement is considered by many as a proof of truth. What it most probably suggests, however, is not truth but a common source. What follows are a number of these common New Age practices and techniques as well as many of the beliefs which seem to flow from them.

Reincarnationists believe that individual souls are recycled over and over again in new human or animal bodies. Each person's present station in life, whether privileged or poverty stricken, results from their actions in former lives (Karma). For them, "Salvation" means to escape the laws of Rebirth and of Karma by uniting oneself with the absolute, but for most souls the future seems to hold only more cycles. It is difficult to see the appeal in these usually endless, dizzying cycles. Especially when the alternative is as simple as following Christ. A Catholic theologian has written a book attempting to reconcile Christian belief with psychic phenomena. He counsels against rejecting the doctrine of reincarnation outright, even though Scripture certainly does reject it. And he considers reincarnation the most plausible explanation for certain cases.[8]

Unfortunately, there are too many such Christians who examine the issue of reincarnation superficially. Certain strange cases seem to them most easily explained by invoking the doctrine of reincarnation. Others seize upon certain Bible verses, taken out of context, to support the concept.

A verse that the reincarnationists like to point to is Matthew 11:13,14. Jesus is speaking of the role of John the Baptist: "For all the prophets and the law have prophesied until John. If you are willing to receive it, he is Elijah, who was to come."

Does this mean that John was Elijah reincarnated? No, what the angel told Zechariah in the temple was that his son John would go out before the Lord "in the spirit and power of Elijah" (Luke 1:17). To go out "in the spirit and power of Elijah" is certainly different from being Elijah and is not without precedent. Elisha's last request before Elijah was taken into heaven was that he would receive a double portion of Elijah's spirit (2 Kings 2:9). No one suggests that Elisha was Elijah reincarnated. When the priests asked John the Baptist: "Art thou Elijah?" he said, "I am not" (John 1:21).

Defenders of reincarnation also quote Jesus' saying, "I lay down my life that I may take it up again. No one takes it from me; I lay it down of myself. I have power to lay it down, and I have power to take it up again." (John 10:17-18). To infer reincarnation from this statement would obviously require sweeping aside Jesus' clear meaning as well as the historical fact of His resurrection. St. Paul wrote, "If Christ is not risen, vain is your faith, for you are still in your sins.... But as it is, Christ has risen from the dead..." (1 Corinthians 15:17, 20).

---

[8]John J. Heaney, *The Sacred and the Psychic: Parapsychology & Christian Theology*, (Paulist Press, New York, 1984) pg 211.

The most familiar "proofs" for reincarnation come from persons who have been hypnotically "regressed" in order to experience supposed past lives. While many such regressions can be dismissed as works of fraudulent showmanship, there are cases concerning persons who describe places they have never been or speak languages they have never learned. Such cases may be explained by the fact that the hypnotist activates long forgotten memories, perhaps from earliest childhood. More ominous still, is the possibility that the subject, in a trance state, is made vulnerable to the influence of demonic spirits. In this event, there is virtually no limit to the wealth of accurate and verifiable "proofs" which might be provided by the spirits in order to convince those eager to be so deceived.

Considered even more convincing are cases in which a young child is believed to recall its previous life. In the typical case, researchers do not arrive on the scene until after the child's recollections have solidified. These children, many from cultures accustomed to the idea of reincarnation, naturally are highly suggestible and subject to the coaching of their elders. Such proofs are thought to be strengthened when the child possesses a deformity or birthmark supposedly relating to the manner of death previously endured. Proponents surmise that the "memory" of dismemberment in a previous life is supported by the fact that a limb is missing in the present life. Reason might offer an alternate explanation. Perhaps it is the missing limb which gives rise to so-called "recollection" of the previous life.

Another theory is that a child's (or adult's) phobias are held to be holdovers from an earlier life. For example, a fear of guns means that a person was previously shot to death. Also, child prodigies who manifest precocious talents in music, arts or sports are said to be the reincarnations of gifted deceased persons. These arguments have the same merit as the birthmark cases. Indeed, Junior's artistic scribbling might cause speculation that he was Michelangelo reborn. So what?

However little or much these cases may seem to prove, it is important to examine what the Church and Scripture teach. Where do souls come from if they are not pre-existent as reincarnationists believe? In the encyclical *Humani Generis*, Pope Pius XII taught "that souls are immediately created by God." From Scripture we learn that souls have never lived before. In Romans 9:11, St. Paul refers to Jacob and Esau, "while they were yet unborn and had done neither good nor evil." Clearly, had they lived before, no one could assert that the brothers "had done neither good nor evil."

We also know that the soul has a destination immediately upon death. As Dr. Ludwig Ott summarizes it in his benchmark work *Catholic Dogma:* Pope Benedict XII, in the dogmatic constitution *Benedictus Deus* (1336), taught that the completely pure souls of the Just immediately after death, or after their purification enter heaven, become partakers in the immediate vision of the Divine Essence, and are truly blessed, while the souls of those in mortal sin immediately enter hell, and are subject to the torments of hell.[9]

Moreover, Scripture tells us: "it is appointed unto men to die once, and after this comes the judgment" (Hebrews 9:27). The Apostle's creed declares, "I believe in...the resurrection of the body, and life everlasting." Neither does the Scripture leave open any provision for reincarnation at a later time. Instead, resurrection and final judgment will occur after the second coming of Christ. Jesus himself warned: "For the hour is coming, for which all who are in the tombs shall hear the voice of the Son of God. And they who have done good shall come forth unto resurrection of life; but they who have done evil unto resurrection of judgment." (John 5:28- 29).

There is no way a Catholic Christian can believe in reincarnation. To do so means to go against both Scripture and the teachings of the Church. It stretches reason. It requires a decision between two absolutely incompatible alternatives: reincarnation and resurrection.

---

[9]Dr. Ludwig Ott, *Catholic Dogma*, pg 475.

The Divinity of Man

When the individual "realizes" his oneness with everything and his oneness with God it follows that he is a full partner in that divinity. This should not be taken in just a philosophic sense. If one is a god he ought to be in control of the universe. Through the occult technique of visualization the practitioner believes that he does in fact create his own universe, continuously. Imagine having such power! Imagine using it! That is exactly what the New Agers would have us do.

Even the business world is learning the value of false pride as a motivator and the benefits of using altered states of consciousness as a "technology" for creating change. Companies as diverse as Pacific Bell, Proctor & Gamble, TRW, Ford Motor Company and Polaroid have signed up New Age consultants or started up training courses in New Age thinking. In the forefront is Werner Erhard—of *est* fame—who has founded Transformational Technologies, "a business designed to do for companies what *est* did for individuals." Transtech fees totaled $15 million in 1986.[10]

New Age training techniques are very appealing to corporate managers because they bypass the employees' reasoning faculties by means of the meditative state. These techniques—self-hypnosis, meditation, centering, visualization, guided imagery and yoga—facilitate the goal of the training, which is to get everyone thinking alike (called "getting aligned"). It sounds good if you don't mind letting someone else think for you. It sounds good unless you object to having yourself initiated into the whole demonic New Age system.

More than one rebellious employee has allegedly been fired for his refusal to participate in New Age training programs and a number have been to the courts for relief. Pacific Bell was immersed in controversy in 1987 as the California Public Utilities

---

[10]*Newsweek*, May 4, 1987, "Corporate Mind Control" pg 38-39.

Commission undertook an investigation of its New Age training program called "Kroning."[11]

In the high pressure, high stress business world well meaning managers are always looking for ways to become more effective. Superiors or co-workers are always pushing numerous different "tape series" or books for self-improvement.

One of the earliest and most influential of the success motivation/positive mental attitude gurus is Napoleon Hill. His book, *Think and Grow Rich*, is a staple in the business world. In it he teaches the sorcerer's techniques of meditation and visualization to create wealth and success. In Hill's lesser known book, *Grow Rich With Peace of Mind*, he explains that these techniques were revealed to him by disembodied Ascended Masters. He writes:

> Now and again I have had evidence that unseen friends hover about me, unknowable to the ordinary senses. In my studies I discovered there is a group of strange beings who maintain a school of wisdom....
>
> The School has Masters who can disembody themselves and travel instantly to any place they choose...to give knowledge directly, by voice....
>
> Now I knew that one of these masters had come across thousands of miles, through the night, into my study....
>
> I shall not set down every word he said...much of what he said already has been presented to you in the chapters of this book and will follow in other chapters.
>
> "You have earned the right to reveal a Supreme Secret to others," said the vibrant voice. "You have been under the guidance of the Great School.... Now you must give the world a blue print...."[12]

---

[11] *Ibid.*

[12] Napoleon Hill, *Grow Rich With Peace of Mind* (Ballantine Books, 1967), pp 158-160 [as quoted by Dave Hunt, *The Seduction of Christianity*, pp. 18-19].

This "blueprint" is the formula around which all the business success/motivation materials revolve. These materials are so much like one another that a single description would cover most that have ever been produced.

It was shortly after I had become aware of the New Age movement that I began to look into some of the so called "success" tapes that I had been listening to. One day, I happened to be traveling with my boss when he brought up the subject of an upcoming promotion review panel which one of my managers would be attending. It would, of course, be very important for the manager to present himself well if he were to be selected for promotion. The boss handed me a book (the name of which I have since forgotten).

"Here is a book I'd like you to give to Dennis to read before the promotion review board. I read it right before I faced the board and it works!"

I began to flip through the pages. The introduction promised a changed life if only I would follow the principles revealed in the following pages. Chapter Two got down to business as it began with the concepts of self-hypnosis and visualization. I shut the book to play a game with the boss. I said:

"I've never seen this book before but I'll tell you what it says. I'll bet it starts with special relaxation exercises where you begin either lying down or sitting erect in a chair and begin to imagine each part of the body as it becomes totally relaxed."

"That's right!" he said.

"Next," I went on, "It tells you to imagine, to picture in your mind, yourself in that particular situation in which you want to find yourself. If you want to be rich, see a picture of yourself as rich. If you want power and success, see yourself as successful and power-ful. Visualize the new car that you want. Whatever it is, visualize it as if it was already yours, believe it, and do it daily. You will bring it about through the power of your mind."

He was shocked. "How did you know?"

"Let me finish." I said with a pride I ought not to have had. "Finally, somewhere in here it says that you are in absolute complete control of your life and everything connected with it. In effect, it says that you are God."

At this point he nearly drove off the road as he reached for the book to show me the last chapter. I read the page where he directed me. It said that I was now ready for the real secret. I read the words: YOU ARE GOD! Now even I was a little unnerved, as my game was more on target than I had imagined. I told him that I was a Catholic and if I were to recommend the practice of Catholicism as a means to prepare for a review board I would probably be called down for it. The contents of his book was just as much a religion as mine, only this was an amalgam of Eastern mysticism, voodoo and witchcraft.

He protested that it works and that it really gave him the confidence to win out at his promotion review. I agreed with him, because, after all, one ought to be completely confident if they believe they are a god. But what will happen when that first inevitable failure occurs and the whole fragile fraud comes down? If one is a Christian he is confident not because of personal greatness but because "I can do all things through Christ who strengthens me."

My boss was quiet for a while and then took back the book saying that he could see now that he should never have shown it to me. Our conversation turned to another subject.

The divinity of man was the key idea taught in Werner Erhard's *est* (Erhard Seminars Training). John Denver, graduate of *est*, and follower of the Swami Muktananda, said of his two mentors: "They're running the universe. They're gods and they know it."[13] About his own future Denver said: "I can do anything. One of these days I'll be so complete I won't be a human. I'll be a god."[14]

---

[13]Newsweek, Dec. 20, 1976, pg 66.
[14]*Ibid.* pg 68.

The guru is worshipped as a god by his followers and he thrives on it. The pleasures of pride are as irresistible to him as they were to his father the devil:

> How art thou fallen from heaven, O Lucifer, who didst rise in the morning? And thou said in thy heart:
> "I will ascend into heaven,
> "I will exalt my throne above the stars of God,
> "I will sit in the mountain of the covenant...
> "I will ascend above the height of the clouds;
> "I will be like the Most High."
> But yet thou shalt be brought down to hell, into the depth of the pit!   (*Isaiah 14:12-14*)

C.S. Lewis called Pride the great sin: "According to Christian teachers, the essential vice, the utmost evil, is Pride. Unchastity, anger, greed, drunkenness, and all that, are mere flea bites in comparison; it was through Pride that the devil became the devil: Pride leads to every other vice: it is the complete anti-God state of mind"[15]

One day, I was tuned into a Christian radio station. My ears perked up as the speaker assured me: "It doesn't matter who you are, Christian or not, nothing is a greater barrier to happiness today than low self-esteem."

"Really?" I thought, "Nothing is a greater barrier? Not even the fact that one is lost?"

The lady preacher continued on, bludgeoning the beast of low self-esteem with the club of human pride. Although appeals to pride seem most shocking coming over a Christian radio station, it does not seem at all incongruous in light of today's human potential movement.

There is scarcely a more universally accepted maxim in today's culture then that most individuals' unhappiness and psychological

---

[15]C.S. Lewis, Mere Christianity, (Macmillan, New York, 1979) pg. 94.

problems stem from low self-esteem. Just as well accepted is the supposed cure for the problem: Build that low self-esteem up. They say that children (and adults) need acceptance, achievement, success and so on. Since we have no lack of good advice and psychological opinion, the list is long. Is meeting the demands of such a laundry list the solution to the problem of low self-esteem?

First of all: What is low self-esteem? Is it seeing oneself as a verminous, useless creature? On the other hand, one might just as well argue that the person with "low self-esteem" thinks not too little of himself, but too much. The unhappiness comes from the inability to compete with the impossible expectations created by pride and an overinflated view of self. Cult expert Dave Hunt disagrees with the notion that all would be well if we could only learn to love ourselves. He says that we love ourselves already:

> Of course, there are many who express varying degrees of self hatred. That they don't actually hate themselves can easily be seen. The person who says, 'I'm so ugly, I hate myself!' doesn't hate himself at all, or he would be glad that he was ugly. It is because he loves himself that he is upset with his appearance and the way people respond to him. The person who grovels in depression and says he hates himself for having wasted his life would actually be glad that he had wasted his life if he really hated himself. In fact, he is unhappy about having wasted his life because he loves himself.[16]

How *should* we see ourselves? An exalted view of oneself is not the answer, for that is the foulest sin of all. Then again, low self-esteem is certainly a miserable state, itself created by human pride which has been twisted and tormented by personal failure and the want of love. What then? Many would say one should have a "healthy self-respect." That's good. But it does not move us

---

[16]Dave Hunt, The Seduction of Christianity: Spiritual Discernment in the Last Days, (Harvest House Publishers, Eugene, OR 1985 pg 199.

toward knowing what a "healthy self-respect" is, nor does it tell us how to get there.

Dave Hunt helps us with the answer as to the proper status of the self:

> The Bible says that we were created in the image of God (*Genesis* 1:26). What do you think of when you think of an image? The first thing you think of is a mirror. A mirror has one purpose and one purpose only and that is to reflect an image other than its own.... Now what would you think of a mirror that tries to develop a good self image? ...We got problems, folks. If there is something wrong with the image in the mirror, what the mirror needs to do is to get back in the right relationship with the One whose image it was designed to reflect. But instead of that we're being turned to self, instead of to Him. Self-confidence, Self development, Self improvement...Self *ad nauseam.*
>
> A young person who gets up in a high school speech class and his knees knock and he stutters and he can't say what he's trying to say...what did we call that person? Self-conscious, right? What's that person's problem? They're thinking of themselves.[17]

The cure for low self-esteem is not to build up one's pride. The remedy is the same as for high self-esteem, that is, no self-esteem. Why be dwelling on the self at all? When the relationship with God is right, all other relationships—including with oneself—are right. It is that condition which gives perfect assurance, yet "in humility, lets each one regard others as his superiors..." (Philippians 2:3).

Contrast this with the New Age goal to become gods ourselves. Many are already convinced. They believe that eventually everyone will be. Meanwhile, they work and wait and meditate, confident that the dawn will yet come for most of the rest of us.

---

[17]Talk by Dave Hunt, Counter Cult Conference, May 26,1984.

Evolution

Darwin was not the first to teach the theory of evolution. This ancient belief is an absolute article of faith and central to New Age—Modernist thought. Man is perfectible and thus divinity is our collective destiny. We are supposedly moving toward what the Jesuit priest, Pierre Teilhard de Chardin, called the Omega Point. In his view, matter has struggled throughout the millennia becoming increasingly complex, ultimately giving birth to humankind. Only the final step awaits us as we are lured on toward unity with "OMEGA" or God.

The recent view of the Catholic Church has been cautious. In *Humani Generis,* Pius XII, permitted discussion of evolution, but warned against any presumption that evolution had been proven true, "as if there were nothing in the sources of divine revelation which demands the greatest moderation and caution in this question."[18] Pius XII's caution was justified; since his death the theory has had some resounding problems.

Despite evolution's scientific mantle or the latest court decision, the theory is proving increasingly faulty with each passing decade. In light of the New Agers' preoccupation with personal experience, evolution may be the only belief that New Agers take on faith. And it must be taken on faith because it has never been observed to occur and the scientific evidence needed to support it does not exist.

When Darwin's *Origin of Species* was published, paleontology was in its infancy, the fossil record as yet unexplored. The years have been cruel to the theory of gradual evolution. The process of naturally selection requires a slow, progressive period of development; a period during which the evolving organism, throughout successive generations, grows legs or wings or whatever.

---

[18]Pius XII, *Humani Generis,* 36.

There are two problems here. One is that the fossil record shows no gradual development from lower organisms to higher. Rather, it shows that species remain generally unchanged throughout time. Those represented in the most ancient fossils are basically indistinguishable from their descendants living today. The fossil record shows creatures that suddenly appear in the world, without apparent ancestors. Some become extinct, while others survive unchanged. The theory demands that there should be transitional forms between evolutionary developments; some sort of creature destined to become a bird whose forepaws are halfway toward becoming wings. Yet, such transitional forms are lacking.

The second problem is the supposed mechanism by which evolution is powered. Mutations (which do occur, but are nearly always detrimental) cause changes in the organism and those which are favorable are retained through natural selection. How then, does a lizard evolve a leg into a wing? After all, what is the advantage in half a wing. Nature might well select for the ability to fly thus preserving this lizard-turned-bird—but how did the lizard ever survive three million years while he was dragging around forelimbs no longer fit for fighting or running but not yet able to lift him in flight?

These problems have not been lost on the evolutionist. Since the only alternative to evolution is special creation, several new concepts have been beaten out to preserve this article of faith.

The Second Law of Thermodynamics, known as the entropy law, states that for all closed systems matter and energy may change in one direction only. That is, from useable to unusable, from concentrated to scattered, from ordered to disordered. In other words, the entropy law states that everything in the universe began with structure and value and is moving irrevocably toward chaos and waste. Automobiles rust out; cities crumble; people age and die. Even a child can see it. It is as much a fact as anything we know.

Enter the evolutionist with a new idea. Call it synergy or syntropy—the built-in tendency toward greater order in nature. Matter just naturally "wants" to perfect itself. Now syntropy, as so far defined, cannot substitute for natural selection. Remember, the fossil record doesn't show gradual formation of species. Syntropy, therefore, must have another curious property: It doesn't operate continuously. Massive evolutionary changes are hoarded within the whole community and are only released in bursts at times of stress. Like an electrical capacitor storing up a charge until finally loosed in a short span, a population of agitated monkeys in part of the jungle rapidly evolves into a tribe of gorillas. This happens so quickly, geologically speaking, that it appears that the gorillas appeared from nowhere. This concept of evolution surging and jerking like a cold engine on a winter morning is called "punctuated equilibrium".

If all this seems a ridiculous construction I can only note that this is taken very seriously by the scientific community. One professor of paleobiology has written about how fortunate it is that the theory of punctuated equilibrium came along just in time to pull the evolutionists' collective fat from the fire.[19]

More fuel was recently added to the debate when geneticists announced the discovery that every human on the planet had descended from a single woman. During the 1960's it was learned that certain parts of living cells—other than the nucleus—contain DNA which is the hereditary blueprint for cell structure and metabolism. These parts of the cell, called mitochondria, produce the cell's energy and are inherited only from the mother. Since this mitochondrial DNA is not scrambled up each generation by mixing with the father's genes, it can be used to trace family relationships. It turns out that human mitochondrial DNA, while different from the apes, is very much alike even across racial and cultural lines. Such differences as exist have been attributed only to genetic mutations.

---

[19]Steven M. Stanley, *The New Evolutionary Timetable* (Basic Books, Inc. New York 1981) pg. 165.

The scientists made molecular comparisons between many individuals' mitochondrial DNA and, assuming a constant rate of mutation, were able to theorize that we all have a common mother who lived about 200,000 years ago. This finding has been upsetting to the traditional anthropologists. While the 200,000 year figure could be off by a 100,000 years or so, it cannot be stretched to fit the 10 million year evolutionary timetable which they had in mind. If that were not bad enough for them, the geneticists have even given our mitochondrial mother a name: "Eve." Still hard at work, the geneticists are confident that in the future they will also discover "Adam."[20]

And yet, the evolutionists stand firm. Nothing will shake their ageless creed, because the alternative, special creation, is unacceptable. Its champions will substitute shamelessly what ever oddly shaped theory they can force into the round hole of the observed facts. It is a matter of faith. Christians believe by faith also, except that there is no need for such tortured theories. Scripture tells us: "I am the Lord, and there is none else: there is no God besides me. I made the earth: and I created man upon it: my hand stretched forth the heavens, and I have commanded all their host." (Isaiah 45:5, 12).

The impact of this undiscerning faith in biological evolution on the broader beliefs of the New Age will become even clearer in chapter four.

Law of Avatars

The beginning of every "New Age" is supposedly initiated by the incarnation of a "god" into a physical body. This *avatar* is a human being who is dominated by the spirit of "The Christ." This century has seen its share of candidates for the office of Christ.

---

[20]Newsweek, January 11, 1988, "The Search for Adam and Eve," pp. 46-52.

Some have been unknown, some have been merely laughed at, while one, the German dictator Adolph Hitler, came murderously close to the goal.

On April 25, 1982 a full page advertisement appeared in major newspapers all around the world. This incredible ad read:

THE WORLD HAS HAD ENOUGH... OF HUNGER, INJUSTICE, WAR.

IN ANSWER TO OUR CALL FOR HELP, AS WORLD TEACHER FOR ALL HUMANITY,

THE CHRIST IS NOW HERE.

HOW WILL WE RECOGNIZE HIM?

Look for a modern man concerned with modern problems—political, economic and social. Since July, 1977 the Christ has been emerging as a spokesman for a group or community in a well-known modern country. He is not a religious leader, but an educator in the broadest sense of the word—pointing the way out of our present crisis. We will recognize him by his extraordinary spiritual potency, the universality of his viewpoint, and his love for all humanity. He comes not to judge but to aid and inspire.

WHO IS THE CHRIST?

Throughout history, humanity's evolution has been guided by a group of enlightened men, the Masters of Wisdom. They have remained largely in the remote desert and mountain places of the earth, working mainly through their disciples who live openly in the world. The message of the Christ's reappearance has been given primarily by such a disciple trained for his task for over 20 years. At the center of this "Spiritual Hierarchy" stands the World Teacher, *Lord Maitreya*, known by Christians as the *Christ*. As Christians await the Second Coming, so the Jews await the *Messiah*, the Buddhists the *Fifth Buddha*, the Moslems the *Imam Mahdi*, and the Hindus await *Krishna*. These are all names for one individual. **His presence in the world guarantees there will be no third World War.**

WHAT IS HE SAYING?

"My task will be to show you how to live together peace-fully as brothers. This is simpler than you imagine, My friends, for it requires only the acceptance of sharing."

"How can you be content with the modes within which you now live: when millions starve and die in squalor; when the rich people parade their wealth before the poor; when each man is his neighbor's enemy; when no man trusts his brother?"

"Allow me to show you the way forward into a simpler life where no man lacks; where no two days are alike; where the Joy of Brotherhood manifests through all men."

"Take your brother's need as the measure for your action and solve the problems of the world."

WHEN WILL WE SEE HIM?

He has not yet declared his true status, and his location is known to only a very few disciples. One of these has announced that soon the Christ will acknowledge his identity and within the next two months will speak to humanity through a worldwide television and radio broadcast. His message will be heard inwardly, telepathically, by all people in their own language. From that time, with His help, we will build a new world.

WITHOUT SHARING THERE CAN BE NO JUSTICE;
WITHOUT JUSTICE THERE CAN BE NO PEACE;
WITHOUT PEACE THERE CAN BE NO FUTURE.

Thus ran this bold advertisement. The "Christ," of course, did not appear in two months or even in two years. Even if such a miraculous appearance did occur, there could be no doubt about his identity. The "Christ" here is not to be confused with Jesus. In this teaching Jesus was one of many "Christs" who have come upon the earth. The Bible is very clear in identifying the nature of any teaching concerning the identity of Christ: "Who is the liar? He who denies that Jesus is the Christ. He is the antichrist, denying the Father and the Son." (1 John 2:22).

Shortly before He was crucified, the Apostles asked Jesus what would be the sign of His coming and the end of the world. He said:

> Take care that no one leads you astray. For many will come in my name saying, "I am the Christ!" and they will lead many astray. Then if anyone say to you, "Behold, here is the Christ," or "There he is," do not believe it. For false christs and false prophets will arise, and will show great signs and wonders, so as to lead astray, if possible, even the elect. (*Matthew* 24:4, 5, 23, 24)

New Age Practices: Yoga, TM & Visualization

New Age meditation includes a variety of related techniques. These are often very similar to the practices of the Hindu and other Eastern religions. Frequently the same practices are, in western civilization, grouped under the heading of *occultism*. The term is one of pride to the occultists, because it means "hidden." These occult or "hidden" powers of the "ancient wisdom" have supposedly been preserved by the "ascended masters" throughout vast ages of time. It is only in the past hundred years or so that many of these "occultists" have been allowed (by their masters) to write and speak of the ancient wisdom.

Yoga, born in the east, is widely practiced in the west. Movie stars do it. Athletes and artists do it. Priests, nuns, and even an American archbishop do it. The Hindi word "yoga" comes from the two sanskrit words "yo" and "ga." Yoga means unity. The goal of yoga is to unite man with the pantheistic God of Hinduism.[21] This union requires a heightened state of consciousness or awareness

[21]Suresh Chander Verma, *Satanic Foundations of Hinduism* (Jesus Christ Trust, Independence, MO, 1983) pg 6.

during which the yogi realizes his oneness with God or the "higher self." It is oneness with God.

It is being God. As such, it is salvation from the Hindu perspective: No sin. No guilt. No savior.

There are a number of types of yoga. Most popular in the west is *Raja* yoga. It is done through meditation and specially designed postures which facilitate the change in consciousness. *Hatha* yoga is the form of yoga which deals with these postures and exercises. It is Hatha yoga which is so often defended as a reliable route to physical fitness. Its advocates often insist that it has no religious aspect that anyone—atheist or Christian—could object to.

Books about Hatha yoga emphasize strengthening the body, increasing flexibility and endurance, as well as reducing tension. The exercises consist of a series of movements, interrupted by motionless "holds" in the various positions. Even the books that steer away from the spiritual side of yoga refer to balancing the "life force" so that body, mind and spirit are in harmony.

The positions can not be brushed aside as mere exercises. They were devised long ago for the practice of Hindu meditation and cannot be safely appropriated by Christians. An example is the well known lotus position. Once the practitioner is seated on the floor, he pulls his legs in close to the hips, with feet resting on the opposite thighs. With the back and head erect and the thumb and index finger pressing together, this position is nearly guaranteed to quiet the mind, slow the breathing, and create a perfect stage for meditation. The erect back and head serve to align the mythical energy centers or *chakras*, while the forefinger thumb contact supposedly prevents the "life force" from dribbling out. Hatha yoga breathing exercises, such as alternate nostril breathing, supposedly balance this mysterious *prana* or "life force."

However much western yoga practitioners wish to pass off yoga as a non-religious system the spiritual nature of Hatha yoga is unavoidable. The ancient *Hatha Yoga Pradipika* records that it was the god Shiva "who expounded the knowledge of Hatha yoga, which like a staircase leads the aspirant to the high pinnacled Raja yoga." The author insists that Raja yoga and Hatha yoga are part of one whole, indispensable to one another. Those who try to separate them, "waste their energy fruitlessly."[22] Sri Aurobindo also taught that every path of yoga, including Hatha yoga, have the same goal—unity with the Supreme.[23]

Transcendental Meditation is the meditative system popularized by the famous guru to the Beatles and others, Maharishi Mahesh Yogi. Called the "Science of Creative Intelligence," this method is Hindu meditation parading as science, notwithstanding its adherents' constant claims that "this is not religious."

The student pays his money, receives preparatory instruction and is interviewed by the instructor. Before the actual meditation is taught the instructor performs a short ceremony designed to thank and honor the chain of meditation teachers ending with the Maharishi's own Guru Dev. They insist, "This is not a religious ceremony." The ritual is performed with various objects—white handkerchief, fruit, and flowers—which the student has brought to the ceremony. It is performed by the teacher and witnessed by the student, ("not religious" they still insist).[24] The student is given his secret *mantra*, a Sanskrit word which is repeated during meditation. The meditator begins by concentrating on the mantra only, which is used to drive out all else. Eventually, even the mantra itself disappears from consciousness. Only nothingness or what is called "pure consciousness" remains. The meditation is practiced for 20 minutes twice each day.[25] This state of consciousness bears no relationship to Christian meditation or what is often called con-

---

[22]*Hatha Yoga Pradipika, Sacred Books of the Hindus* (Sudhindranatha Vasu, Allababad. India, 1915) pp 1, 27, 58.

[23]Sri Aurobindo, *On Yoga I: The Synthesis of Yoga* (Sri Aurobindo Ashram Press, Pondicherry, India, 1957) pg 601.

[24]Nat Goldhaber, *An Alphabetical Guide to the Transcendental Meditation Program* (Ballantine Books, New York, 1976) pg 215.

[25]*Ibid.*, pg 51-52.

templation. This will be more fully explored in the chapter on "The New Age Mystic." Advanced courses are also available and in these the religious character of TM is more apparent. The yoga techniques of posture and breath control are used. The goal is the same.[26] This is not to say that the sellers of TM are lying when they say it is not religious. What they mean is that it involves no teaching of dogma and no overt reference to God. It is a technique.[27] This is true. What is not said is that while the dogma is not taught, it will be learned. The changes in one's spiritual perspective and worldview come through the use of the technique. One need not hear the word "Hindu" in order to become one. The United States Third Circuit Court of Appeals is also convinced that SCI/TM is a religion. They upheld a lower court decision bouncing TM classes out of the New Jersey public schools, calling it "an establishment of religion."[28]

TM has made incredible claims for itself. A former teacher has sued TM, claiming that the organization promised that in the "Sidhis" course he would learn to "fly" or self-levitate. More over, he alleged that he damaged his legs while trying to "fly" (i.e., hopping around in the lotus position) and that he was "permanently psychologically damaged as a consequence of practicing TM."[29] TM's newspaper advertisements offer *increased* intelligence, concentration, memory, creativity, athletic performance and more.[30] If this were not spectacular enough, how about this ad which the Maharishi's World Government of the Age of Enlightenment ran in *The Wall Street Journal* on August 19, 1983:

---

[26]Kenneth Boa, *Cults, World Religions, And You* (Victor Books, Wheaton, IL, 1977) pg 158.

[27]Goldhaber, *Alphabetical Guide,* pg 182.

[28]Malnak *v.* Yogi, 592 F.2d 197 (1979).

[29]Doe *v.* Yogi, 652 F. Supp. 203, 209 (D.D.C. 1986).

[30]*The Maneater*, February 16, 1988, pg 13.

GOVERNMENTS
INVITED

TO SOLVE THEIR PROBLEMS. THE WORLD GOVERNMENT OF THE AGE OF ENLIGHTEN- MENT ANNOUNCES its readiness to solve the problems of any government regardless of the magnitude and nature of the problem—political, economic, social, or religious; and irrespective of its system—capitalism, communism, socialism, democracy, or dictatorship.

Governments are invited to contract with the World Government of the Age of Enlightenment to solve their problems.... Complete confidentiality is assured....[31]

TM is just one of many doorways to the altered states of consciousness essential to New Age thinking. Whether the meditative mental state is brought about by Hindu meditation or yoga or even through self-help tapes or books teaching self-hypnosis, the effect is the same. Even the use of drugs may have the same effect as these techniques. The mind is opened up to influences which no human can control.

Visualization is the meditator's attempt to manipulate the world around him. The technique involves a self-induced trance and the use of the imagination to picture a particular result in the mind (more on this later). A related technique is called guided imagery, in which the meditator is gently guided by spoken words into a hypnotic trance. Guided Imagery is more a beginner's technique often used on children and dispensed with once the student becomes more "advanced." It is commonly used on New Age "self-help" tapes and is frequently combined with New Age music to facilitate the meditation. Both visualization and guided imagery make this use of imagination. That is not to say that there is anything wrong with the common use we make of the imagination

---

[31]*The Wall Street Journal*, August 19, 1983, pg 19.

in our everyday life. Dave Hunt makes the distinction in his book *Beyond Seduction*:

> It should be clear that remembering a person, place or event from the past involves mental imagery—and it is just as harmless (and beneficial) to use the imagination to plan something in the future such as a house one hopes to build. Nor is there anything wrong with mentally rehearsing the delivering of a speech or practicing one's golf or tennis swing in the mind. As soon, however, as we think that visualization somehow creates or influences exterior reality (i.e. visualizing the golf ball dropping into the cup will make it happen) or that contact can be made with Jesus or God, we have opened ourselves to possible demonic influences.[32]

Visualization is probably the single most important New Age technique. It is the action side of the movement. Whereas simple meditation purports to *know*, visualization *does*. Without visualization, our material-minded western society would lose patience with mere meditation. It is the promise of power that lures business people to practice visualization. The same practice that the African "witch doctor," the Siberian *shaman* and the traditional witch rely upon is promoted for the healing of illness, for consulting with spirit "counselors" and to gain material wealth.

There is no Church tradition or Scripture to support the practice of visualization. We are not commanded to go within and create God in our imaginations. Rather "faith is the substance of things to be hoped for, the evidence of things that are not seen." (Hebrews 11:1). God has condemned divination and sorcery as the tools of the false prophets: "The prophets prophesy falsely in my name: I sent them not, neither have I commanded them, nor have I spoken to them: They prophesy unto you a lying vision, and

---

[32]Dave Hunt, *Beyond Seduction: A Return to Biblical Christianity*, (Harvest House Publishers, Eugene, OR 97402, 1987) pg 198.

divination, and deceit, and the seduction of their own heart." (Jeremiah 14:14).

We have good cause to reject the technique of visualization. It is deceptive and dangerous. But what if it were not? How can one answer the New Ager whose only response is: "It works!" Leaving one's fate in God's hands is not just obedience; it is wholly practical, for in doing so we choose the greater over the lesser. We trust His visions; not ours. St. Paul reminds us that Christ "is able to accomplish all things in a measure far beyond what we ask or perceive." (Ephesians 3:20).

Clearly, even if man *could* create his own reality; even if he were his own god, he must naturally fall short of the glory and happiness which God has in store for him. Dull, weak and colorless by comparison, the universe of the man/god must be limited by his own puny, wicked imagination. He's eating bologna when he should be eating steak. A motto of the New Agers is, "Whatever the mind can conceive, it can achieve." That is exactly the problem.

New Age Miscellany: Crystals, Rainbows, Channeling, Holistic Health

I will conclude this overview with an assortment of popular New Age ideas and symbols:

Crystals are the real "Pet Rocks." Many New Agers believe in crystal power. Quartz crystals are believed to focus energies in the body, to amplify, balance and harmonize. Other crystals and gemstones of different types and colors are thought to have different effects so that a well-equipped crystal devotée may have a jade for wisdom and tranquillity, a sapphire to elevate the mood and a carnelian to stimulate curiosity. One must learn though, which crystals complement each other and which should be worn alone. This is, however, no more scientific than astrology and, even if harmless, the use of crystals is just one more rejection of God as the answer for man's spiritual problems.

The *rainbow* is the symbol of God's covenant with men and beasts that He would never again destroy the earth in a flood.

(Genesis 9:12-17). In the New Age, this meaning is discarded and the rainbow has become a symbol of the movement. It is known as the *Antahkarana* or Rainbow Bridge and represents the bridge of consciousness that each must build between his own mind and soul and the universal mind and soul. It symbolizes realization of oneness with the universe.

One day I was browsing through the gift shop at Unity Village, Missouri near Kansas City. Unity Village is an important New Age center and many Unity people visit there on vacation, perhaps on a pilgrimage of sorts. I overheard a woman next to me admiring a striking crystal shaped like a prism which when placed in a window would spray a rainbow of color across the room. She wanted it, but her husband said, "I thought you said you wanted something that would have real meaning." With that, the woman took him by the arm and pulling him out of earshot gave him (I assumed) the short course on crystals and rainbows. They bought the crystal.

The importance of symbols is more than just to let New Agers find each other. Symbols are used to aid meditation. A person who has learned to meditate with a certain mantra or by using a particular image or place of meditation (real or imagined) will find that the meditation aids will enable him to easily and quickly achieve an altered state of consciousness. Some other New Age symbols are triangles, circles, the sun, crescent moon, and stars—five pointed, especially upside down—or the star of David, because of the dual triangle structure. There are also the dragon, the unicorn and other mythical creatures; rays of light, the oriental ying/yang symbol, the swastika, enneagram and various perversions of the cross such as the Egyptian anhk and the upside down cross. Even the number of the Beast of Revelation "666" is found woven into New Age logos.

I want to caution the reader that while the New Agers use these symbols, they don't own all of them. Many are legitimate Christian symbols. Some people just like pretty crystals. A rainbow sticker in the back window doesn't necessarily mean a New Ager is meditating at the wheel. I once asked an employee of mine what her purpose was in hanging a rainbow from her rear-view mirror. "It's an air freshener," she said, "Keeps the car from stinkin', Why?"

A few years ago hardly anyone would have known what a *trance channeler* was. Now anyone who saw Shirley MacLaine's TV movie "Out on a Limb" not only knows what channeling is but witnessed a real trance channeler go into a self-induced trance to enable a spirit being to take over his body. The channeler is what has been called a trance medium in the past. They allow supposed disembodied "ascended masters" to take control of their voice and body and then communicate with onlookers. The messages from these beings are blasphemous toward God and thoroughly New Age in their teachings. If these spirits are genuine then trance channeling can only be a demonic phenomenon.

It is interesting that *most* New Agers, even the most extreme like witches—absolutely reject the notion that they follow Satan. And yet, they gladly take marching orders from more "evolved" beings. With the true scheme of things being as it is, what a shock to find out—too late—that Satan, ruler of hell, is the most "evolved" being of them all.

The *Holistic (or Wholistic) Health movement* is based on the premise that a person must be seen as a whole being; body, soul (or mind), and spirit. That, in itself, is no revelation. Clearly, the mental and spiritual life affect—and are affected by—the physical body. The problem with the overwhelming bulk of so-called "holistic health" practices lie in the treatments employed to cure the problems on the spiritual side:

- Acupuncture and accupressure (designed to balance the vital energies supposedly coursing through the body and certain energy centers or "chakras" as the occultists call them).
- Yoga and Transcendental Meditation
- Psychic Healing and Therapeutic Touch
- Use of Crystals and Color Therapy
- Nutritional therapies based on the supposed spiritual properties of foods.

The obvious reaction to such a list must be that these spiritual "treatments" are not for Catholics. Where is the Catholic list, the one with the prayers, sacraments and Scripture reading on it? Needless to say it does not exist. Even if it did, few health professionals would be qualified to apply it. This brand of holistic health is more than a harmless fad. It is spiritually dangerous.

Finally, it would not do to end this chapter without mentioning the mellow music of the New Age. New Age music seems to come in three levels. At the worst, there is the droning hypnotic deep-toned variety. It is distinctive because, in spite of the absence of drums, there is a heavy beat or OM chant running throughout. The mental effect is to induce a hypnotic trance. It works. It leaves one feeling rather dazed and dulled. I have heard Christians who are former New Agers say that it makes them feel seduced and filthy, almost as if they had been molested. On a spiritual level that is a good analogy of the effect upon a Christian.

On the next level, the music is more like a smooth flight above the clouds or a sailboat on a mirrored lake. Usually very pleasant, these synthesized sounds are often blended with natural sounds such as rain or songbirds. The purpose seems to be relaxation; and while the sounds are very congenial to meditation, the corrupting hypnotic beat of the first type is missing. Still, these are not fit for Christian consumption, whether one intends to meditate or not. The problem is subliminal suggestion. Many New Age artists use subliminal messages which are not consciously heard. This is not conjecture. Some albums not only state that the music contains subliminal messages but will tell the listener what the messages are. Here are a few real samples:

- "You are a channel for the light."
- "You invoke the blessing of the source of the light."
- "Up, up, higher, higher, fly with me"

or for specialized purposes:

- "The psychic power you desire is within you and is yours by divine right."
- "You stick to your diet."

The selling point here is that a subliminal message will not be filtered through the rational mind but instead finds it way inside uninhibited. If subliminal messages work one can become a New Ager without having made any conscious choice other than to listen to relaxing modern "elevator" music. This "middle" type of New Age music may actually be more spiritually damaging than is the first sort, if only because it is disarming.

The third sort of music does not *seem* to be New Age music at all. It sounds normal; it has melody; it goes somewhere during the song and then comes back at the end. It may be that even New Age musicians just get sick of the mindless pabulum they usually play and every once in a while stick in a real tune. Or perhaps the record companies, knowing that New Age music sells, get a little over-zealous in attaching the "New Age" label. The safest course, however, is to stay away from all of it.

2.

Education in the New Age

The theme of the 1985 National Catholic Education Association convention was *Gateway To Global Understanding*. Selected to deliver the keynote address was Robert Muller, at that time Assistant Secretary-General of the United Nations. Promotional literature also listed his name along with the likes of humanist-astronomer Carl Sagan, New Age networker Robert Theobald and several other Globalism/New Age Education advocates. My interest and surprise were sufficient to motivate my registration and attendance at the conference.

The first afternoon Robert Muller set the tone for the meeting. After a number of highly flattering opening remarks he observed that Jesus gave us a universal view because he had come from outer space. Muller reminded the educators that the purpose of the whole conference was for them to implement a global curriculum. He said there was a "need to design a core curriculum for every Catholic school on this planet. I have written such a global core curriculum" he said.

Muller's Curriculum

Muller's "core curriculum" can be found in the July/August and September/October 1982 editions of *The Beacon*, which describes itself as a "magazine of esoteric philosophy, presenting the principles of the Ageless Wisdom as a contemporary way of life." *The Beacon* is the bi-monthly publication of the openly occult Lucis Trust. Muller organizes his curriculum around the categories of the universe, the human family, our place in time and, lastly, "the miracle of individual human life."[1] The goal, he says, "is to make each child feel like a king or queen in the universe, an expanded being aggrandized by the vastness of our knowledge...."[2] Muller wraps up his global curriculum with a call for good physical, mental, moral and spiritual lives. A good spiritual life he defines as having "spiritual exercises of interiority, meditation, prayer and communion with the universe and eternity or God."[3]

Listening to Muller, it sounds like religion class will never be the same again. One thing I do not recall from my years in the Catholic school was my first "Communion with the Universe." Robert Muller is worth a closer look, especially since his books can be found on the shelves of most Catholic bookstores. Muller's latest book, *New Genesis: Shaping a Global Spirituality*, raises some important questions about this man and why he should be seen as the embodiment of the values that we as Catholics hope to bring into our schools.

His message is that global education must go beyond material, scientific and intellectual achievements and encompass the moral and spiritual spheres. Specifically, the job of global education is to prepare our children for the coming of an interdependent, planetary age, which has supposedly been foretold by all the great prophets.[4]

---

[1]Robert Muller, *The Beacon* (Lucis Publishing Company, NY July/August 1982) pg 299.

[2]Robert Muller, *The Beacon* (Lucis Publishing Company, NY September/October 1982) pg 331.

[3]*Ibid.* at 332.

[4]Robert Muller, *New Genesis: Shaping a Global a Spirituality* (Image Books, Garden City, NY, 1984) pg 8.

Muller considers himself a good Catholic but believes that one religion is as good as another. He says: "You are born into a religion and it will give you full satisfaction. Be interested in all religions, in what they have in common, but there is no compelling reason to switch."[5]

Muller had never been deeply religious, so it was not until he became assistant to the late U Thant, Secretary-General of the U.N., that he was inspired to see life and spirituality bound inextricably together. Buddhist U Thant, whom Muller calls his "spiritual master," caused him to take up the study of Buddhism in order to understand the man better.

"I would never have thought that I would discover spirituality in the United Nations!"[6] he wrote. That "spirituality" as explained in his book, *New Genesis*, is found in the pantheistic religions of Buddhism or Hinduism. He gives us a view of God as a force, a "cosmic" force which is indistinguishable from the universe as a whole. The supposed effect of this force is to exert upward evolutionary pressure upon all mankind to realize that they are divine; that they are God. We have only to realize this great truth. Judge for yourself how well his written word squares with traditional Christianity:

> [O]ur planet, all life on it, and in particular human life, is a manifestation of cosmic or divine forces of the universe. Within us therefore resides a basic cosmic force that impels us to respond to our evolutionary duties....[7]
>
> Humankind is seeking no less than its reunion with the "divine," its transcendence into ever higher forms of life. Hindus call our earth Brahma, or God, for they rightly see

---

[5]*Ibid.* at xiii.
[6]*Ibid.* at 171.
[7]*Ibid.* at 136.

> no difference between our earth and the divine. This ancient simple truth is slowly dawning again upon humanity.[8]
>
> We must elevate ourselves again as light, cosmic beings in deep communion with the universe and eternity. We must re-establish the unity of our planet and of our beings with the universe and divinity ....We must see our planet and ourselves as cells of a universe which is becoming increasingly conscious of itself in us. That is our royal road out of the present bewilderment.[9]

Muller's syncretistic groping gives us a "cut & paste" system in which Christianity puts in only a cameo appearance. There is a danger here in proclaiming the equality of all religions. The problem is well expressed by James Hitchcock:

> The religious traditions of the world were to [the devotées of popular religion] like a marvelous tree laden with ripe fruits. They were free to pick and enjoy whatever fruits struck their fancy, to leave those that seemed slightly bitter, and above all never to worry about where the tree came from or how it was nourished and maintained.[10]

It was an incident concerning a man, a woman, a serpent and another fruit laden tree that was the beginning of our rebellion. That unhappy episode ended with the man and the woman being driven from paradise. God cursed the serpent for his role and ordained a future of toil, suffering and sorrow for mankind. This was perhaps the darkest day in human history. Why is it then that Robert Muller exults in the shame? He writes:

> We can elicit pride at being humans, at being able, above all species to go so far in the universe....

---

[8] *Ibid.* at 49.

[9] *Ibid.* at 37.

[10] James Hitchcock, *What Is Secular Humanism* (Servant Books, Ann Arbor, Michigan, 1982) pg. 79.

> [H]aving decided to become like God...we have also
> become masters in deciding between good and bad....[11]

To Muller, it seems, the fall of man turns out to have been a big plus. If we had not chosen to become like God we would have not realized our destiny: to become a showcase in the universe, a planet of God.

Muller's idea's are drawn in part from Teilhard de Chardin. In fact, he has entitled one chapter of his book "My Five Teilhardian Enlightenments" in which he tells the remarkable tale of how he came to hold Teilhard's view of the world. It seems Muller fell into his philosophy as he observed the world through his vantage point at the U.N. At various speaking engagements Muller would find himself blurting out certain ideas of Teilhard such as that "the human species was entering...a period of planetary consciousness" or that he viewed "the earth as a 'living cell.'" At some point he would realize (with all appropriate humility) that he had experienced his own "Teilhardian Enlightenments" without benefit of Teilhard himself.

Muller's ideas have proven popular with New Age groups such as the Arcane School and World Goodwill. World Goodwill distributes one of Muller's speeches from June, 1989 in which he reminds us where his loyalties lie. Muller advises: "love the planet and humanity above anything else." But what does Scripture teach? "Do not love the world," says St. John the Apostle (1 John 2:15). Rather, "Thou shalt love the Lord thy God with thy whole heart, and...soul, and...strength, and...mind; and thy neighbor as theyself" (Luke 10:27). World Goodwill and the Arcane School are affiliated with Lucis Trust, whose publishing branch was originally incorporated as the Lucifer Publishing Company. This openly occult organization is based mainly on the writings of Alice A. Bailey whose books (she claims) were dictated to her telepathically by the

---

[11]Muller, *New Genesis* at 145.

Master Djwhal Khul who supposedly inhabits the high places in Tibet.

The goals of Lucis Trust include the establishment of a new world order, a new world religion and a new world leader. In their literature this is known as *the plan.*

The plan is directed by so-called "higher intelligences" or "the hierarchy." Robert Muller seems to be perfectly comfortable with these masters of wisdom as he once told the Arcane School how modern science is verifying the proclamations of these "outer space emissaries."[12]

In another speech Muller spoke on the "New Group of World Servers: A Look Into The Future." The New Group of World Servers' role is to prepare us for the New World Christ. Lucis Trust describes the role of the world servers in the May-June 1983 issue of *The Beacon*:

> Their work is intended to open up the way to the hierarchy and act as a channel through which can flow the new energies. This, in turn will open up a clear channel for the spirit of peace…. [T]his agent of interplanetary love [will] be overshadowing and working through the Christ when he appears….[13]

It should be pointed out that when occultists use the term "Christ" they actually refer to "Lucifer." David Spangler is a board member of the Planetary Initiative For the World We Choose, a grandchild of Robert Muller's Economic and Social Council of the United Nations. Spangler, more than anyone else, has been open about the identity of the "cosmic" forces that Muller so eagerly serves. He writes in his book, *Reflections on the Christ:*

---

[12]*Ibid.* at 121.

[13]Dale McKechnie, *The Beacon* (Lucis Publishing Company, NY May/June 1983) pg 77.

> Christ is the same force as Lucifer....
>
> Lucifer prepares man...for the experience of Christ-hood....
>
> [A]s we move into a new age...each of us in some way is brought to that point which I term the *Luciferic Initiation*, the particular doorway through which the individual must pass if he is to come fully into the presence of his light and his wholeness.
>
> Lucifer comes to give us the final...Luciferic initiation ...that many people now and in the days ahead, will be facing, for it is an initiation into the New Age.[14]

And finally, Muller has left a hint concerning the origin of his fruit-laden tree in the conclusion of his book *New Genesis:*

> And God saw that all nations...were sending their emissaries to a tall glass house...on the island of Manhattan....
>
> And God said: That is good. And it was the first day of the New Age of the earth.
>
> And God saw that the soldiers of peace were separating the combatants of quarreling nations....
>
> And God said: That is good. And it was the second day....[15]

This recital continues quite predictably. Throughout all seven days (not six), we humans brilliantly eradicate hunger and ignorance, waste and bigotry. On the seventh day God and man together are restored as the *Alpha* and *Omega* and what we'd always thought was a throne turns out to be a love seat. Never mind, God obligingly scoots over and announces that, this too, is good. As mankind basks in its self-generated glory, Muller puts these final words in God's mouth:

---

[14]David Spangler, *Reflections on the Christ* (Findhorn, Scotland, 1978) pp 40-44.
[15]Muller, *New Genesis,* pg 190.

I will now make My peace with you and let you establish a
perfect Earth. Farewell, My grownup children. At long last
you are on the right path, you have brought heaven down
to earth and found your proper place in the universe. I will
now leave you for a long journey, for I have to turn my sight
to other troubled and unfinished celestial bodies. I now
pronounce you Planet of God. Be happy. [16]

Now I don't know how Robert Muller's Bible ends but mine
does not have God riding off into the sunset. As I read the above
passage it struck me first as being just some more typically sac-
charin New Age rubbish. And then...no; far more fitting are these
words in the mouth of Satan, spoken at that moment of final ruin.
He fancies himself corrupting other worlds when he has finished
with ours. My Bible disagrees on this point also. Satan's end is
clearly pictured in the prophetic book of Revelation: "And the
devil who deceived them was cast into the pool of fire and
brimstone, where are also the beast and the false prophet; and they
will be tormented day and night forever and ever." (Revelation
20:9, 10).

Robert Muller has every right to believe whatever he wishes
and to spread his cosmic, global gospel. The question is what are
Christians doing fooling around with such nonsense? And how long
will we tolerate the feeding of the lie to our children?

National Catholic Education Association

If the 1985 convention stood alone as an aberration, it might
not be worth a closer look. But the movement in education did not
begin in 1985, nor is it over now. Even a sympathetic New Age
source admits that the effort to undermine the nation-state system
and implement global thinking goes back at least fifteen years:

---

[16]*Ibid.* at 191.

The NCEA launched a "Peace Education" program in 1972 which seeks to develop a global consciousness among its member educators, thus laying the basis for developing a planetary framework for integrated curricula development.[17]

If the only questionable speaker at the 1985 NCEA convention had been Robert Muller, then it would hardly be worth a fuss. Unfortunately, Muller was only a fragment of the picture, albeit an important one.

One speaker was John I. Goodlad, who presented "Restructuring the Educational Process." From the outset, he assumes that Catholic parents will not like "global education." In the forward to James Becker's book, *Schooling for a Global Age*, Goodlad cautions:

Parents and the general public must be reached also. Otherwise, children and youth may find themselves *in conflict with values assumed in the home.* And then the educational institution frequently comes under scrutiny and must pull back.[18]

Carl Sagan, of COSMOS fame, insulted every Catholic in the house during his talk about "nuclear winter." Notwithstanding the fact that true Christians have always been willing to die for their faith, the surprise was that Sagan was applauded when he suggested that no religion (or political belief) was worth dying for.

Another very popular speaker was Dolores Leckey, Executive Director of the U.S. Bishops Committee on the Laity. The preliminary convention program described her as:

[A] great spokesperson for every Catholic woman...someone whose spirituality and sense of meaning has been

---

[17]Gerald and Patricia Mische, Toward a Human World Order, (Paulist Press, New York, NY/ Ramsey, NY 1977) pg 308.

[18]James Becker, *Schooling for a Global Age* foreword by John I. Goodlad, (McGraw Hill, New York, 1979) pg xvii (emphasis added).

strongly shaped by her Catholic roots, but who has dared
to explore other sources of wisdom as well...a typical
female Catholic of the '50s who broke the mold.

In her speech to the general session, she approvingly cited
writer and lecturer Rosemary Haughton, saying: "She is pointing
to the new physics...and to the wisdom of the east as a means of
recovering that which has been lost...a new alternative social
order."

I always sit up straight and listen when Christian speakers defer
to the "wisdom of the east." She began to explain how Jesus was
able to work his healing miracles: "He [Jesus] perceived in others
the operation of the same divine energy that was his own motive
power. He knew people...as possessing the same power he had."

Leckey further explained that when Jesus told someone that
their faith had healed them:

> He was acknowledging the power of the transaction, a
> flowing of knowledge and power between them. His com-
> passion was an essential agent, it is true, yet one that was
> powerless, in a sense, without the response that somehow
> completed the circuit and transformed the situation. Jesus
> found himself able to liberate the divine energy in people
> over and over again. When he did this it produced a
> psycho-physical transformation that came neither from
> him nor from the other person. It was not isolated in that
> way, but was the fruit of their encounter.... [T]hough it
> seems at times that he tried to contain the phenomenon...it
> simply couldn't be done.

According to Leckey, it was as if Jesus were a mere man who
happened to find "himself able to liberate the divine energy," who
couldn't "contain the phenomenon," and was powerless without
the "response that...completed the circuit." But faith is not power.
It is not even half of the power. If that were so, then how did Jesus
raise the dead? Certainly a dead body has no faith. At the pool of
Siloam the man born blind made no expression of faith but instead
seemed to serve purely as a demonstration of the power of God.

It is the belief of those who practice the so-called "mind powers" that faith is power in itself. In effect one must have faith in his faith. But faith must have an object, and more, that faith must be in the correct object. Someone has said that given the problem of crossing a deep gorge, one would do better crossing a strong bridge though frightened and unsure of its strength than to cross a fatally-weakened bridge with confidence. If the object of faith is correct, the faith will be rewarded.

At another session, New Age author Robert Theobald spoke about "The New Technologies and Global Education." His talk was concerned with the ways he felt we must all change in the future, how we must teach "holistically" and teach "values." Before leaving the convention I picked up a little volume called, *At the Crossroads*, at a booth attended by Sister Judith Bisignano (more on this interesting lady shortly). Although the book was authored by a committee, the sister told me that Theobald was the chief writer. *At the Crossroads* turns out to be a New Age manifesto. Just a few of the concepts embraced:

- subordination of the needs of nations to needs of the planet
- interdependence and connectedness of all things
- government by an elite few
- visualization
- development of new governmental boundaries

The document is signed by many New Age notables and the list of recommended resources is loaded with New Age references:

- Marilyn Ferguson's *Leading Edge Bulletin*
- Mark Satin's *New Options* newsletter
- Marilyn Ferguson's *The Aquarian Conspiracy*
- John Naisbitt's *Megatrends*
- Donald Keys's *Earth at Omega*
- Peter Russell's *The Global Brain*
- Fritjof Capra's *The Turning Point*

Kino Learning Center

One last example will serve to complete this short review of this NCEA convention. Sister Judith Bisignano, O.P., Ed.D., offered the blatant "A Working Model of New Age Learning." Sister Bisignano is the founder of the Kino Learning Center of Tucson, Arizona. The Kino Learning Center, Inc. is a Catholic elementary and secondary school founded in 1975. The sister spoke mostly about the New Age philosophy that she and her colleagues bring to the school and how Kino puts that philosophy into action. She appealed to the teachers present to take the lead in bringing in the New Age. She began with her opinion that:

> Children are an oppressed minority, and certainly Catholic schools have the ability, have the freedom...to be leaders of ...the new age model.
> Things have to change drastically...If this happens.... Catholic schools will become a major leader in the regeneration of society.

A few traditional skills (like reading and writing) are required for graduation, but for the most part students at Kino are free to learn only what they wish to learn--or to learn absolutely nothing: "Children should have the freedom to do nothing," the sister told us. This is called a "child-centered" classroom. Someone asked the question whether the children must learn certain truths such as the Resurrection. Sister Bisignano said, "If the topic...doesn't interest him then he's not going to learn about the Resurrection."

She says that if the child doesn't *choose* to study it in her school then neither would he learn about it in a conventional class room. A question concerning the teaching of the Ten Commandments was asked and sister answered:

"If the child is not interested in the Ten Commandments today, then he doesn't have to learn them. The power is in the child to direct his life."

"But is it possible," asked one teacher, "that the child might never learn the Ten Commandments?"

The answer was affirmative: "You could get through Kino without choosing to study the Ten Commandments."

The sister was not apologetic. Instead, she seemed to lament the fact that they were required to teach certain things (such as reading and the other basics). She confessed that she herself hated to read, considered it pure drudgery, and felt that the day would soon come when the children needn't learn to read at all. In the meantime though, Kino does provide the opportunity to read.

She said what she really wanted was to teach the values that would hold the children in good stead in the New Age. These values were taught through a series of workbooks which she proudly displayed on the dais. Sister Bisignano longed for the day when those workbooks would be all that needed to be taught. One workbook, *Living With Death*, exposes the student to the concepts of suicide and euthanasia without giving them real guidance as to the right and wrong of it. One project has the student writing a "living will" in which the student proclaims that death is preferable to the "indignities" of illness and demands "mercifully administrated" medication "to alleviate suffering even if it may hasten the moment of death."

Other exercises involve the student in visiting mortuaries, writing out the funeral invoice for his own burial, designing tomb stones, writing obituaries, donating organs and doing death crossword puzzles (*hint:* 12 DOWN is reincarnation).[19]

One page dealt with life after death. It explained that many people believe that each person (and sometimes animals, plants, rocks and rivers) have a spirit within:

> Some people believe that the soul goes to a spirit land, sometimes called Paradise or Heaven, where perfect happiness exists. Some people believe that a spirit leaves a dying person and enters the body of a baby that is being

[19]Judith Bisignano O.P., Ed.D., *Living With Death* (Sheed & Ward, Kansas City, MO 1985) pp 36-41, 46, 48, 50-55.

born. Other people believe that a human spirit finds a home in some animal--a bird, a cow, or a dog. These beliefs of a spirit living again in another person or animal are called reincarnation.

If you believe in life after death, use words and pictures to describe what you think this might be like.[20]

The bottom half of the page was left open for drawing whatever the student wished. The exercise did not suggest which view was the correct one.

Another Kino workbook, *Creating Your Future*, has a foreword by Robert Theobald. The opening and closing exercises are tests of the students' awareness and acceptance of New Age concepts taught in the workbook. In between are lessons designed to induce fidelity to a New Age platform (global consciousness, a new world order, the doctrine of unlimited human potential).[21]

None of the above was done in a vacuum. Present at the conference were several American archbishops, including Milwaukee Archbishop Rembert Weakland. While there was no lack of criticism of the agenda, unfortunately none of it came from the archbishops. The organizers of the event dismissed all dissent as coming from a narrow-minded minority. Sister Mary Ann Eckhoff, superintendent of schools for the archdiocese of St Louis, explained the rationale: "We may not agree with everything we hear [at the conference], but we don't grow up in a cocoon....Catholic educators are sophisticated enough to sift out truth."

"[T]eachers who attend the NCEA meeting will just have to sort out for themselves what is poisonous and antithetical to Catholicism and what is not," explained one editorial.[22]

---

[20]*Ibid.* at 33.

[21]Judith Bisignano *et al, Creating Your Future: Activities to Encourage Thinking Ahead,* (Kino Learning Center, Tucson, AZ, 1985) pp iii, 1, 35, 61.

[22]*The Wanderer,* April 18, 1985 (Wanderer Printing Co. St Paul, MN) pg 4.

For several years following the 1985 convention, the New Age themes cut a narrower swath at NCEA conventions. The globalist/New Age presentations became inconspicuous, and were limited to the workshops. Whenever there are *useful* workshops to attend, few teachers willingly show up in these New Age sideshows. To reach the teachers, the New Agers need the captive audience of the convention's general sessions to effectively communicate their message. Being stuck in the workshops is a high hurdle for the New Agers to overcome when the general sessions are encouraging authentic Catholic teaching and basic fundamentals.

Unfortunately, the New Age found its opening again with the address of Jean Houston, Ph.D. to the 1989 NCEA convention. Dr. Houston, founder of The Foundation for Mind Research, spoke in the general session.

Dr. Houston is past-president of the mystical/occult-oriented Association of Humanistic Psychology and a member of the International Advisory Board of the Oasis Center of Chicago, Illinois. The Oasis Center's holistic schedule includes programs on Yoga, Shamanism, Healing Touch, I Ching, and the "Goddesses in Everywoman."[23] In 1988, the center offered Houston's own seminar: "Pangaia: Whole System Transition and the Earth's New Story: A Mythic Event."[24] Jean Houston has co-authored the book *Mind Games*, a series of group explorations into altered states of consciousness. Scattered throughout the book are graphic images accompanied by the words WAKE UP! Houston explains that the "mind games" in the book (intended for group sessions) will also induce a trance in some readers. Readers wishing to terminate the trance need only look at the image, clap hands and say "WAKE UP!" In this book, Jean Houston teaches the sorcerer's techniques

---

[23]*Oasis Center*, January-March, 1989.
[24]*Oasis Center*, July-September, 1988.

of visualization and even materialization of an entity she calls "the Group Spirit." This entity, which is conjured up during a deep group "shared trance," is described as perceptible to all the senses, including touch. The "players" establish a rapport with the spirit entity which takes and answers questions.[25]

She has predicted "that in our lifetime we will see the rise of essentially a new world religion.... I believe a new spiritual system will emerge...."[26] Jean Houston has recounted how, as a young girl, she was influenced in her talks with an elderly man she called "Mr. Teller." Only later did she learn that the man she had befriended as a schoolgirl in New York City's Central Park was Pierre Teilhard de Chardin.[27]

Undoubtedly there are individuals within the NCEA still dedicated to spreading the New Age infection to the Catholic schools. As long as New Age luminaries such as Muller and Houston are welcomed by NCEA the contest will not be won. One thing is certain; those fouled with the New Age creed will not go quietly. The prize is too big.

The underlying motive behind this push for the Globalist-New Age agenda stems from the unique position occupied by the Catholic Church. In a real sense--and Robert Muller said as much in his keynote address to our Catholic school teachers--the Church is the big prize. The Catholic Church, with its worldwide school system, has been targeted as the most potent vehicle possible in bringing in the New Age. The prize is not unwinnable, because while the Church will remain in some form until the second coming, that does not insure that the decay will not be far advanced. And

---

[25]Robert Masters and Jean Houston, *Mind Games* (Viking Press, New York 1972), pp. 198-206.

[26]Texe Marrs, *Dark Secrets of the New Age* (Crossway Books, Westchester, Illinois, 1987) pg 40, quoting Jean Houston, interviewed in "Jean Houston: The New World Religion," The Tarrytown Letter, June/July 1983, pg 5.

[27]Muller, *New Genesis*, pg 167-68.

to whatever extent the Church is itself preserved, it is not churches who rebel. It is not the Church to whom Jesus will say, "Depart from me," but to individuals. Eternal life, while won by the death and Resurrection of Christ, is chosen by individuals, one at a time. There has never been an age for serene, witless indifference; and ours is no exception. There is no guarantee of safety in the modern church's arms; no assurance from Scripture that God will protect a stubborn and corrupted people from the movement which threatens to overtake and swallow it.

The Local Catholic School

There has been much talk about the shortage of vocations and the increasing importance of an active laity. Every parent should be involved with what their children are learning in school. It does not take long to look over a religion textbook. Look for minimizing of the deity of Christ and distortions of the fact of sin; look for the equating of Christianity with all other religions; or worse the actual criticism of Christianity in comparison to the so called "higher" religions of Hinduism and Buddhism. While you are looking, notice what is not there: The authority of the Church and the Scriptures, the reality of heaven, hell and purgatory, the fact of the biblical miracles and a general lack of guidance for the child's moral growth. A Catholic textbook for older students needn't ignore other religions but there is an obligation to point to the truth. A "neutral" lesson is not neutral at all, because it teaches that all religions are equal. That is not Catholicism. That is the New Age religion. Talk to your children to find out what they are doing in religion class. William C. Brown Company, the same publisher that brought us the widely (and properly) criticized elementary sex education series *New Creation*, has produced *Guided Meditations for Children*, written by Jane Reehorst, B.V.M. Subtitled, "How to Teach Children to Pray Using Scripture," the meditations are recommended for use with the "Light of Faith" series also from Wm. C. Brown. These meditations use "guided imagery," a form of visualization. At first, the technique looks like simple story telling, but it is much more.

The teacher allows the children to choose body positions which will establish their commitment to prayer and will be conducive to comfort and relaxation. The teacher is encouraged to begin with the meditation, "Meeting Jesus." This establishes that place in the child's imagination where he can go to meet Jesus whenever he wishes. This same device is used in the Silva Mind Control Method (see chapter seven) to facilitate meditation and visualization. Silva calls this special place the "laboratory." For the rest of the school year the "prayer" time is begun with the words, "Let us go to our place to meet Jesus." The class is encouraged to go to that place whenever they want.[28] A meditation begins: "Close your eyes (pause) Take a deep breath (pause) and relax (pause) You are walking with Jesus and his disciples...." The teacher "guides" the children through the experience. They play with Jesus. He talks. The child talks and plays. All of this is like a story until abruptly the teacher says, "I'll leave you alone with Jesus to begin your game of celebration." And just like that the teacher saws off the limb and the child is left alone with his visions. You can see that "guided imagery" is guided only to a point. After a time the teacher says a prayer and tells the children, "It is time to leave.... Say goodbye to Jesus.... and begin to walk away.... Open your eyes and come back to the room."[29] The children are back from their hypnotic trance but there is one more New Age chore to perform before finishing. The children finish each meditation by writing down their responses to these visualizations of Jesus.[30] If it were not enough that the children are initiated into guided (and unguided) meditation the

---

[28]Jane Reehorst, B.V.M., *Guided Meditation: How to Teach Children to Pray Using Scripture* (Wm. C. Brown, Dubuque, Iowa, 1986) pg vi.
[29]*Ibid.* at 11.
[30]*Ibid.* at vi.

text the teacher uses is three-fourths fantasy. Subtle distortions come in. At the wedding feast at Cana, the child is present and sees Mary come up and speak to Jesus. Later a servant brings wine, apologizing for the delay. "For awhile we thought we ran out of wine," he says "but now we have plenty."[31] That scene has meaning for you and me, but then we know the story. Too bad the child doesn't get the point.

During another meditation, the child finds himself at the feeding of the multitudes. Jesus says "Pass this out to the people," so the child and the apostles begin to pass out the loaves and fishes but there is a discrepancy: "Soon your bread is gone." Jesus shares his food with the child. There are twelve baskets of food left over. The lesson: "When one shares God's gifts there is always enough to go around."[32] Once again you have to get the feeling that someone is hiding the ball here. Is it necessary to paper over the obvious miracle that occurred in order to teach children to share?

If your child is exposed to New Age ideas and meditations in school you are the one that must do something. Talk to the pastor. Talk to the school board. Talk to the bishop. You may be surprised by the appreciation of those unaware of the problem. On the other hand, be prepared to be ignored, or worse, insulted. Some parents have been not so politely told to shut up or get their children out of the school. But these are our children and there is no one else to stand up. Very likely it is the lay person, the parent and courageous Catholic school teachers who must take up the challenge and withstand the attack of those who would use and then destroy the Church. Power is not measured by the letters after one's name, but by obedience to God. The battle is not hopeless. As the Apostle Paul reminds us:

> For the rest, brethren, be strengthened in the Lord and in
> the might of his power. Put on the armor of God so that

---

[31]*Ibid.* at 10.
[32]*Ibid.* at 25-27.

you may be able to stand against the wiles of the devil. For our wrestling is not against flesh and blood, but against the Principalities and the Powers, against the world-rulers of this darkness, against the spiritual forces of wickedness on high. (Ephesians 6:10-12)

3.

Priest or Guru?

It is a common question: Why do people (especially religious and clergy), when they no longer believe in the faith they espouse, insist upon remaining in and influencing the Church? Not that every Catholic holds exactly the same belief on theological matters, but there are essentials of belief which one must accept or reject. To deny these essentials should mean to relinquish the name "Catholic" or even "Christian." C.S. Lewis once gave a speech to an assembly of Anglican priests and youth leaders. He asked them to respect the boundary lines:

> I think it is your duty to fix the lines clearly in your own minds: and if you wish to go beyond them you must change your profession.
>
> This is your duty not specially as Christians or as priests but as honest men. There is a danger here of the clergy developing a special professional conscience which obscures the very plain moral issue. Men who have passed beyond these boundary lines in either direction are apt to protest that they have come by their unorthodox opinions honestly. In defence of those opinions they are prepared to suffer obloquy and to forfeit professional advancement. Thus they come to feel like martyrs. But this simply misses the point which so gravely scandalizes the layman. We never doubted that the unorthodox opinions were honestly held: what we complain of is your continuing your ministry after you have come to hold them. We always knew that a

man who makes his living as a paid agent of the Conservative Party may honestly change his views and honestly become a Communist. What we deny is that he can honestly continue to be a Conservative agent and to receive money from one party while he supports the policy of another.[1]

All we should ask is that when a Catholic, especially one with a teaching office, chooses to become (for example) more Hindu than Ghandi, that he have the courage and honesty to quietly dissociate from the Church.

Is it possible that the most "Christian" view is one that admits that all religions are paths to God? Certainly that seems the most loving, open and kind interpretation. But it can do no good to insist that all paths lead to God if, in fact, they do not. It is Jesus Himself who declares:

> Enter by the narrow gate. For wide is the gate and broad is the way that leads to destruction, and many there are who enter that way. How narrow the gate and close the way that leads to life! And few there are who find it! (Matthew 7:13, 14)

So-called open-minded people rail against the "one way" view point that true Christianity teaches and in doing so they reject Jesus' sacrifice.

Before Christ's death all mankind was lost to sin, separated from God by an impassable gulf. It is as if Jesus came to build a bridge over which everyone could cross. Even though He paid the highest possible price to build that one bridge there are those who insist that He build innumerable others. They would accuse God of cruelty if He were to punish people who refuse the provision

---

[1] C.S. Lewis, *God in the Dock* (William B. Eerdmans Publishing, Grand Rapids, MI, 1970) pg 90.

made by Jesus Christ. *Cruel* is a better description for these open minded ones who, in effect, would crucify Jesus again and again.

We have been commanded to "make disciples of all nations, baptizing them in the name of the Father, and of the Son, and of the Holy Spirit" (Matthew 28:19). The tragedy is that so many religious no longer see this as their commission. They work to change the world when they ought first be working to save souls. This pattern, typical of popular ideas today, is not the biblical one. Instead, the truth is made a lie as the proper sequence is inverted; our order of priorities has become perfectly and completely reversed. The world says: take care of material needs first. Only then can spiritual needs be met. Jesus says: "But seek first the kingdom of God and his justice, and all these things shall be given you besides." (Matthew 6:33).

In an article from *America* magazine, Denis Murphy reported on a new way to look at evangelism. From the Cardinal of Karachi, Pakistan: "Conversions are not the most important...Rather our task is to give an extraordinarily clear witness to our Christian values, especially in social matters of justice and honesty."[2] A bishop in Bangladesh says, "Islam and Hinduism are salvific, for how could the good God abandon them." Even in the sharing of his faith he says he does it because he values the faith, not because the pagans needed it.[3]

Using the most convoluted, useless logic possible, an Indian Jesuit theologian argues that, "the fact that members of the higher religions, such as Hindus and Buddhists, do not convert may be a sign that they are not meant to convert."[4] One might as well conclude that the fact that a man is starving may be a "sign" that he wasn't "meant" to eat.

---

[2]Denis Murphy, *America* (August 25,1979).
[3]*Ibid.*
[4]Denis Murphy, *America magazine* (August 25, 1979) pg 75.

These are the modernists of our day and like those condemned eighty years ago by Pius X in *Pascendi*, they "do not deny, but actually maintain, some confusedly, others frankly, that all religions are true."[5] These arguments of the modernist, are merely unconvincing end runs around such compelling biblical injunctions as the Great Commission or this simple reasoning by St. Paul: "For whoever who calls upon the name of the Lord shall be saved. How then are they to call upon Him in whom they have not believed? But how are they to believe him whom they have not heard? And how are they to hear, if no one preaches? And how are men to preach unless they be sent?" (Romans 10:13-15).

It is the conventional wisdom of the mission fields that the missionary must learn of the ways, language and culture of the people he would convert. The situation in the east has gone a step further, and we find that it is the pagan that has instead converted the missionary. Jesuit priests have started imitating the Hindu holy men, taking the title "swami" and wearing saffron robes and sporting begging bowls. The so-called "Indian rite" uses the mantra "OM," the name of the Hindu god Krishna.[6] Bede Griffiths is one of these Christian gurus.

Bede Griffiths

The initial religious formation of Dom Bede Griffiths O.S.B. was minimally Anglican. Of immense influence upon him was his early reading of the Hindu *Bhagavad Gita* and other books of eastern spiritual wisdom introduced to him by a friend of his mother. This friend, who was to have such a strong effect on him

---

[5]Pius X, *Pascendi*, pg 16.
[6]Malachi Martin, *The Jesuits* (Linden Press, New York, 1987) pg 411.

was a Theosophist and suffragette who shocked children by smoking cigarettes.[7]

Griffiths, once a student of C.S. Lewis at Oxford, converted from unbelief to Catholicism at about the same time Lewis was undergoing his own conversion. He entered a Benedictine monastery within a few weeks of his conversion and was later ordained a priest.

Bede Griffiths had assumed that he would preach the gospel but learned he could not teach that which he was still searching for. He went to India to help found a monastery and never left. His community, called *Shantivanam*, is affiliated with the Benedictine community of Camaldoli in Italy, but follows the customs of a Hindu ashram, with Griffiths as guru.[8] He says: "Certainly from a Christian point of view the importance of Indian philosophy can hardly be overestimated. It marks the supreme achievement of the human mind in the natural order in its quest of a true conception of God."[9]

Griffiths calls the Hindu temple a "sacrament" and is caught up in admiration for these people who have so penetrated the "ultimate mystery." In the temple of Shiva the destroyer, the innermost holy place contains the lingam or phallus where the worshipper communes with the ultimate reality.[10]

He claims that it is easy to meet the Hindu on the level of liturgy, language, music and art, but very difficult to meet him on a theological level. Nevertheless, Griffiths believes that the task is possible. Unfortunately, this is only accomplished by subordinating

---

[7]Bede Griffiths, *The Golden String* (P.J. Kennedy and Sons, New York, 1954) pg 58.

[8]Harrison Hoblitzelle, *New Age Journal,* "A Visit with Father Bede Griffiths: INDIA'S CHRISTIAN GURU", August, 1983 pg 40.

[9]Bede Griffiths, *The Golden String,* at 152.

[10]Bede Griffiths, *Christ In India* (Charles Scribner's Sons, New York, 1966) pg 99.

Christianity to Hinduism. He accuses Christians of having an imperfect understanding of Christ (which may be true), but he then proceeds to send us to Hindus and Muslims to clear up our misunderstandings.[11] In the end he sees no rationale for preaching the gospel for at bottom we are all believers. Father Griffiths says:

> No one can say in the proper sense that the Hindu, the Buddhist or the Muslim is an "unbeliever." I would say rather that we have to recognize him as our brother in Christ....
>
> [O]ur task in India is not so much to bring Christ to India (as though he could be absent), as to discover Christ already present and active in the Hindu soul.[12]

We should not think, however, this phenomenon of priests becoming gurus as only happening halfway around the world. We have our own priest-gurus here in the United States. One is Father Edward Hays who is widely recognized as an expert on prayer.

Formerly a parish priest, he was sent on a year long pilgrimage by his archbishop. Father Hays had requested a few months off for prayer in a Christian monastery, but his bishop, now Archbishop Ignatius Strecker of Kansas City, KS, had other ideas. He suggested that Hays take a year off to travel in search of new ideas: Hays was advised to go also to the non-Christian religions in his quest for freshness in spirituality. The archbishop hoped that Father Hays would found a "house of prayer" upon his return. He traveled to the Middle East and the Orient as a prayer pilgrim seeking wisdom.

For more than sixteen years, Father Hays has run his Catholic-Hindu "house of prayer" which is financially supported by the Catholics of Archbishop Strecker's archdiocese. The name of his

---

[11]*Ibid.* at 183, 189.
[12]*Ibid.* at 196, 217.

retreat house is "Shantivanam" (Forest of Peace), the same as Bede Griffith's ashram in India.[13]

The chapel at Shantivanam is a tiered octagonal room with a decided eastern flavor. We interrupt a young man's yoga meditation as we enter the chapel. The altar (an old wooden horse manger) stands on bare earth facing neat rows of oriental prayer rugs. Lit by candles and sunlight, and scented with incense, the room is a museum of religious evolution.

Father Hays' system is pure syncretism. He blends Christianity with the other religions and puts Jesus in the same class as "Buddha and the other holy saviors...."[14] In a layout reminiscent of the stations of the cross, one side of the chapel holds a shrine to Shiva, Hindu god of destruction. Next on this wall, is a Buddha, followed by a copy of the Scriptures, the Tabernacle of the Blessed Sacrament, a picture of Our Lady of Guadalupe, and finally, a crucifix. The purpose is to give due honor to each progressive revelation. The large windows wrap around one end of the chapel to give a beautiful panorama of the forest and fields. With the wide assortment of gods available here, a worshipper could get confused. Nevertheless, the god of Shantivanam receives her due, because the goddess of Shantivanam is creation. Nature is the theme that claims the field of vision here: the expanse of windows and the altar dug into the dirt. This is creation-centered spirituality.

Hays is typically eastern in his teachings. He recommends the use of a mantra, proper breathing and special sacred places for meditation.[15] Speaking of our "new spirit of sexuality" he says: "We must trust our inner voices even when they assert that there is goodness and beauty in what past ages have called evil and dirty."[16]

---

[13]*The Catholic Key*, KEY Welcomes Fr. Ed Hays As A New Contributing Columnist April 21, 1985).

[14]Edward Hays, *Secular Sanctity* (Forest of Peace Books, Easton, KS, 1984) pg 16.

[15]*Ibid.* at 101.

[16]*Ibid.* at 80.

See how this inverts the words of Isaiah (5:20):

> Woe to you that call evil good, and good evil:
> that put darkness for light, and light for darkness:
> that put bitter for sweet, and sweet for bitter.

In his newspaper columns he has done the same thing: Turning the Scriptures (the Christian Bible) upside down. Most often it is the Oriental scriptures which he quotes, and then with earnest reverence. In one story, Father Hays portrays a king who refuses Heaven unless God lets both his dog and his unbelieving family into heaven with him. The stubborn king wins out and God praises the king's faithfulness, as He allows them all in.[17] Once again the truth is the exact opposite, for Jesus said:

> He Who loves father or mother more than me is not worthy of me; and he who loves son or daughter more than me is not worthy of me. Everyone who has left house, or brothers, or sisters, or father, or mother, or wife, or children, or lands for my name's sake, shall receive a hundredfold, and shall possess life everlasting. (Matthew 10:37, 19:29)

While the flavor of the east dominates Shantivanam the western pagan traditions are not ignored. A former staff member has related that, "On occasion, ancient festivals of the Celts or Saxons are remembered and members dance round a may pole or a fire pit in the fields or forest."[18] Even a druid or a witch could feel at home in a place like this! But pagan idols and Celtic festivals aside, business at this Archdiocesan "house of prayer" is quite good. Shantivanam can barely accommodate visitors from outside the Archdiocese.

---

[17] Edward Hays, *The Catholic Key*, April 21, 1985.
[18] Ron Miller and Jim Kinney, *Fireball and the Lotus* (Bear & Co., Santa Fe, New Mexico, 1987) pg 195 [article by Michael Hugo].

Thomas Merton

This chapter would not be complete without some comment about the man who has been so influential in transforming a key segment of the Catholic church—the contemplative orders. The man is Thomas Merton. He has been described as "an Englishman who became a Communist, then a Catholic, later a Trappist monk, and finally a Buddhist, at which point, his life having been fulfilled, he died."[19] There was little about Merton's life—whether before or after his conversion—that could be called orthodox. He viewed the Catholic life as inducing "all forms of neurosis and anxiety."

"The way the Christian life is lived, he said, is so schizophrenic that it is a wonder one can be at the same time a Christian and sane."[20]

Merton's pre-occupation was with mystical experience. His overreaching assumption was that all such experiences were valid and self-authenticating regardless of their source. To him, the inner journeys of all religions were equally true. Merton wanted to see a synthesis among the religious traditions of the world. Shortly before his death, he wrote an admiring introduction to a new translation of the *Bhagavad Gita*, the most important of the Hindu scriptures.

His last journey was to the Orient in 1968 at the time of the first World Spiritual Summit conference sponsored by the Temple of Understanding. As he departed the U.S., Merton said he left with "a great sense of destiny, of being at last on my way after years of waiting and wondering and fooling around" (remember, Merton had spent the previous 27 years as a Trappist monk at Gethsemani, in Kentucky—apparently, as he wrote, "fooling around").[21]

---

[19] Edward Rice. *The Man in the Sycamore Tree: The Good Times and Hard Life of Thomas Merton* (Doubleday, Garden City, NY 1970) pg 139.

[20] *Ibid.* at 192.

[21] *Time* magazine (August 6, 1973) pg 54.

He spent time in Asia with various gurus including the Tibetan Dalai Lama. Merton gave the closing address to the Conference in Calcutta on October 23, 1968. He told the assembly:

> If [all] are faithful to their own calling...and to their own message from God, communication on the deepest level is possible.... Not that we discover a new unity. We discover an older unity. My dear brothers, we are already one. But we imagine that we are not. And what we have to recover is our original unity. What we have to be is what we are.[22]

His audience was largely composed of non-Christians from all over the world. What did he suggest in saying: "My dear brothers, we are already one?" We are left to figure out whether he had joined his hearers or that his hearers had joined him. Just before his accidental death in Bangkok, on December 10, 1968, he told a gathering of Christian monks and nuns from various parts of Asia: "The monk is a man who has attained or is about to attain, or seeks to attain, full realization. He dwells in the center of society as one who has attained realization—he knows the score.[23]

Time magazine (August 6, 1973) reported that "his death prompted friends to speculate whether Merton would ever have returned to the U.S. from his enthusiastic plunge into Buddhism. The answer now seems to be yes, though he might not have returned to Gethsemani itself."

Some Buddhists revere Merton as a reincarnated Buddha, while one spirit medium reports that Merton has escaped the cycle of reincarnation and is now the Ascended Master "Davog" whose task is to prepare for the second coming of Jesus.[24]

---

[22]William H. Shannon, *Thomas Merton's Dark Path: The Inner Experience of a Contemplative* (Farrar Straus Giroux, New York, 1981) pg 215.

[23]Shannon, *Thomas Merton's Dark Path*, at 216.

[24]Edward Rice, *The Man in the Sycamore Tree*, at 11, 139.

Doubtless, Merton was remarkable. Anyone who captured such interest from Christians, Eastern mystics and occultists would have to be. It is regrettable that he found traditional Christianity so insufficient (and even maddening), feeling instead, the need to look to the east for truth.

Some individuals have dabbled ignorantly in eastern religion. Others are fully aware of what they do. Priests and nuns are teaching Hindu meditation. An American archbishop reportedly does yoga.[25] Thousands of Catholics have been introduced to spirit guides and visualization techniques. They are in danger. They need our prayers.

---

[25]Leon V. King, *The Wanderer,* "Why Rembert Ate Meat," January 22, 1987.

4.

Pierre Teilhard de Chardin

In 1980, Marilyn Ferguson published her book, *The Aquarian Conspiracy: Personal and Social Transformation in the 1980's*. In it, she favorably describes the New Age Movement as:

> A leaderless but powerful network...working to bring about radical change in the United States. Its members have broken with certain key elements of Western thought, and they may even have broken continuity with history.[1]

She describes how new ideas are changing people everywhere: in business, religion, leisure and sports. Ferguson writes:

> It seems to speak to something very old. And perhaps, by integrating magic and science, art and technology, it will succeed where all the king's horses and all the king's men failed.
>
> The transformative process, however alien it may seem at first, soon feels irrevocably right. Whatever the initial misgivings, there is no question of commitment once we have touched something we thought forever lost—our

---

[1]Marilyn Ferguson, *The Aquarian Conspiracy: Personal and Social Transformation in the 1980's* (J.P. Tarcher, Los Angeles, CA, 1980) pg. 23.

way home. Once this journey has begun in earnest, there is nothing that can dissuade. No political movement, no organized religion commands a greater loyalty.[2]

The Hinduistic flavor of much New Age religion is not innately attractive to the Western mind. Its emphasis upon the illusory nature of matter does not come naturally to many of us. The materialism of our society could be a roadblock to the popularity of the New Age movement were it not for the writings of the French Jesuit priest, Pierre Teilhard de Chardin.

It is Teilhard whose work has glorified, rather than denied, the material world. For him, matter is sacred; he made the idea of the "God within" work. Teilhard theorized a synthesis of the spiritual and the material which has had a conspicuous effect not only on many Catholics, but upon "Aquarian Conspirators" everywhere.

In her book, Marilyn Ferguson published a survey of persons involved in "social transformation." These self-proclaimed "conspirators" singled out one man more often than any other. Pierre Teilhard de Chardin was the individual most frequently cited as having had a profound influence upon their thinking. The list headed by Teilhard included a wide range of influential figures including C.G. Jung, Aldous Huxley, Swami Muktananda, Thomas Merton, Buckminster Fuller, Werner Erhard and Maharishi Mahesh Yogi.[3]

It is my intention to shine a critical light on this dead priest's influential teachings and ideas. My hope is that others will be warned away from the real but false appeal contained in his theories.

---

[2]*Ibid.* at 18, 34.
[3]*Ibid.* at 420.

Teilhard and Modernism

In 1903, Pierre Teilhard de Chardin was twenty-two years old and studying for the priesthood when Joseph Sarto, Patriarch of Venice, was elected Pope Pius X. Although Teilhard was too young to come under the scrutiny of Rome at the time of the publication of Pius X's encyclical "On Modernism" (*Pascendi*), he learned well the defensive techniques of his Modernist heroes, for he would use the same hypocritical tactics later during his own difficulties.

Representative of the Modernists' strategy is the case of the French priest, L'Abbé Alfred Loisy. Loisy popularized Modernist beliefs which he had imported from the Protestant liberal theologians of nineteenth century Germany. Notable was his denial of the divinity of Jesus. Michael Davies, in his book, *Partisans of Error*, wrote of Loisy's relationship with and attitudes toward the Church and his superiors:

> St. Pius X had five of Loisy's books placed on the Index in December 1903. Loisy made a reluctant act of submission in 1904, but it was in no way sincere. He wrote in his journal for 10 May 1904: "I remain in the Church for reasons which are not of faith but of moral expediency."
>
> In a letter to Cardinal Merry del Val on 24 January 1904 he stated: "I accept all the dogmas of the Church."…[H]is real thoughts were set down in his diary: "I have not been a Catholic in the official sense of the word for a long time…Roman Catholicism as such is destined to perish, and it will deserve no regrets." In an entry dated 12 May 1904 he states: "Pius X, the head of the Catholic Church, would excommunicate me most decidedly if he knew that I hold…the virgin birth and the resurrection to be purely moral symbols, and the entire Catholic system to be a tyranny which acts in the name of God and Christ against God himself and against the Gospel." Despite all the incontrovertible evidence which proves the insincerity of Loisy and other Modernists, they still have apologists today who depict them as sincere and selfless seekers after truth, noble scholars who fell victim to an ignorant and

unscrupulous clerical bureaucracy. In the Liberal Catholic mythology, Loisy is still the hero and St. Pius X the villain.[4]

Pius X understood the Modernist's attitude toward the church's rejection of their teachings. Some excerpts from *Pascendi:*

> [T]he Modernists express astonishment when they are reprimanded or punished. What is imputed to them as a fault they regard as a sacred duty. For them to speak and to write publicly is their bounden duty. Let authority rebuke them as much as it pleases—they have their own consciences on their side and an intimate experience which tells them with certainty that what they deserve is not blame but praise.
>
> They go their way, reprimands and condemnations not withstanding, masking an incredible audacity under a mock semblance of humility. While they make a show of bowing their heads, their hands and minds are more boldly intent than ever on carrying out their purposes.
>
> And this policy they follow willingly and wittingly, both because it is part of their system that authority is to be stimulated but not dethroned, and because it is necessary for them to remain within the ranks of the Church in order that they may gradually transform the collective conscience.[5]

Teilhard de Chardin was teaching at the Catholic Institute in Paris when he first ran afoul of the Church's teachings. He wrote an essay, not intended for publication, for the purpose of explaining his views on the fall and original sin. In it, he denied the existence of Adam, Eve, Paradise or a time before man had sinned.

---

[4]Michael Davies, *Partisans of Error: St. Pius X Against the Modernists* (The Neumann Press, RR2, Long Prairie, MN 56347, 1983) pp. 70-71.

[5]Pius X, *Pascendi Gregis* (Burns & Oates Ltd., London, 1907) pp. 33, 34.

Eventually Teilhard's essay came to the attention of Church authorities who were forced to react in view of his position as a teacher. Rome demanded that he give up his teaching position at the Institute and that he sign a statement reversing his earlier written position.

Ellen and Mary Lukas explained Teilhard's dilemma in their book, *Teilhard*. His friend and old classmate, Auguste Valensin, counseled him that:

> There was nothing he could do but yield entirely or leave. After considerable deliberation, Valensin decided that Teilhard's best course was to consider the physical action of signing the document as a gesture of fidelity rather than a symbol of intellectual assent, and sign it. Fundamentally, he argued all the Society asked for was obedience. Heaven would judge the rest.
>
> [H]e...put his signature to every proposition Rome demanded—even though, as he wrote Edouard Le Roy, he had not changed his ideas or his sense of mission in the slightest.
>
> "I stand condemned," he once remarked..., "by dolts and ignoramuses!"[6]

This was only the first encounter in a lifetime during which Teilhard's ideas would be repeatedly rejected. A rough chronology of his difficulties runs as follows:

1911: Pierre Teilhard ordained a Jesuit priest.

1920: Teilhard taught at the Institut Catholique in Paris.

1924: His initial troubles began with his essay written earlier in which he denied the fall of man, the existence of Adam and Eve and garden of Eden.

1925: Rome demands he give up Institut teaching position and sign retraction of his views. He signs.

---

[6]Mary Lukas and Ellen Lukas, *Teilhard: The Man, The Priest, The Scientist* (Doubleday, Garden City, NY, 1977) pp. 94-95.

1927: Rome refuses to grant an imprimatur to *The Divine Milieu*

1933: Teilhard is ordered not to teach in Paris and refused permission to publish his book, *Human Energy*.

1937: In May, Teilhard is "ordered by his major superiors to stop disseminating his outrageous ideas..."

1944: His most famous work: the *Phenomenon of Man* is banned. Was refused professorship at College de France.

1947: *Phenomenon of Man* is extensively reworked in order to pass Church scrutiny. Instead, Rome forbids his writing or teaching on any but scientific subjects.

1948: *Phenomenon of Man* is again refused publication.

1949: Teilhard's printings and activities are restricted. He is refused permission to publish *The Human Zoologic Group*.

1951: Lived in U.S. until 1955.

1955: Printings and activities again restricted. Pierre Teilhard de Chardin died April 10, 1955.

1957: Holy Office decree ordering withdrawal of his works from Catholic Libraries, religious institutions and bookstores.

1962: John XXIII issued *monitum* warning against "serious errors" in Teilhard's works.

1981: *L'Osservatore Romano* states that the earlier *monitum* is still in effect.

Teilhard's Theology

Teilhard believed in two kinds of energy inherent in all matter. First of all, there is *tangential* energy. Tangential energy is familiar because it so definitely surrounds us. It is physical energy or what Teilhard would call external or "the without." Subject to *entropy*, tangential energy tends toward disorder or diffusion.

Teilhard theorized a second form of energy he called *radial* energy. This internal energy or "the within" might be called spiritual or psychical energy. Unlike tangential energy, radial energy tends toward complexity. It has purpose or consciousness, thus providing direction for its evolutionary course. In the beginning, this extremely simple consciousness of elemental matter was supposedly sufficient to cause the formation of more complex molecules. This resulting increase of complexity led in turn to a higher level of consciousness. This cycle of consciousness-complexity—higher consciousness—higher complexity is Teilhard's mechanism for evolution.

He seems to suggest that this radial energy or consciousness can be equated with God. It is true that God holds all the universe together for "in him we live, and move, and have our being." And it is not wrong to say that God is immanent—unless one means (as the Modernists mean) that He is only immanent and not transcendent.

To deny that God is transcendent or existing independent of His creation is to say that He is no God at all. Teilhard's God has existence only in matter, for without matter he could not exist. Teilhard wrote in *Human Energy:*

> One is inseparable from the other; one is never without the other; ...No spirit (not even God within the limits of our experience) exists, nor could structurally exist without an associated multiple, any more than a center without its circle or circumference. In a concrete sense there is not matter and spirit. All that exists is matter becoming spirit.
>
> So much matter is needed for so much spirit.[7]

We are supposedly locked into a self-creating system in which matter will ultimately become spirit when the necessary level of both complexity and consciousness have been attained. This increasing "complexity-consciousness" is an upward spiral which has experienced several breakthroughs. This progression—from Pre-Life to Life, from Life to Thought—is to continue to the next stage: That of a superconsciousness where the radial energies of all

---

[7]Pierre Teilhard de Chardin, *Human Energy* (Harcourt Brace Jovanovich, Inc., New York, 1969) pp. 57, 162.

mankind coalesce into a collective human organism stretched over the entire planet.

New Agers are eagerly awaiting this next step but feel it can only come about when a certain critical number of individuals are joined together to bring it about. Teilhard called it the Omega Point. Just like a nuclear chain reaction which can occur only when a certain critical mass of uranium or plutonium is brought together, the jump to Omega will occur only when a critical mass of humanity is ready. This excerpt from Ken Keyes' *The Hundredth Monkey* explains the New Agers' hope:

> The Japanese monkey, *Macaca fuscata*, has been observed in the wild for a period of over thirty years. In 1952, on the island of Koshima scientists were providing monkeys with sweet potatoes dropped in the sand. The monkeys liked the taste of the raw sweet potatoes, but they found the dirt unpleasant.
>
> An 18-month-old female named Imo found she could solve the problem by washing the potatoes in a nearby stream. She taught this trick to her mother. Her playmates also learned this new way and they taught their mothers too. This cultural innovation was gradually picked up by various monkeys before the eyes of the scientists. Between 1952 and 1958 all the young monkeys learned to wash the sandy sweet potatoes to make them more palatable. Only the adults who imitated their children learned this social improvement. Other adults kept eating dirty sweet potatoes.
>
> Then something startling took place. In the autumn of 1958, a certain number of Koshima monkeys were washing sweet potatoes—the exact number is not known. Let us suppose that when the sun rose one morning there were 99 monkeys on Koshima Island who had learned to wash their sweet potatoes. Let's further suppose that later that morning the hundredth monkey learned to wash potatoes.
>
> Then it happened! By that evening almost everyone in the tribe was washing sweet potatoes before eating them. The added energy of this hundredth monkey created an ideological breakthrough! But notice. A most surprising

thing observed by these scientists was that the habit of washing sweet potatoes then jumped over the sea — colonies of monkeys on other islands and the mainland troop of monkeys at Takasakiyama began washing their sweet potatoes! Thus when a certain critical number achieves an awareness, this new awareness may be communicated from mind to mind."[8]

Whether this doubtful story is true or not, it perfectly illustrates the sort of wild-fire shift in consciousness which Teilhard looks forward to. This also explains why we periodically see the advocates of this sort of "super consciousness" getting together from time to time for "planetary healing meditations." They've done this over and over by now, each time without result. The reader may remember the Harmonic Convergence of August 16-17, 1987. Many of these New Age pilgrims traveled to various sacred, planetary "pressure points," while the rest contented themselves with doing their tree-hugging, hand holding, "ooommming" and "aahhhing" in local gatherings. If you don't remember this cosmic event, it's probably because nothing happened except some muffled snickering. Lamented one frustrated advocate: "The media made us look like air-headed idiots."[9] Such failures do not, however, daunt the true believer. There is always next time. The hundredth monkey is out there somewhere. Meanwhile these exercises continue.

Sinful Rocks and Theosophist Roots

This system of Teilhard's is coherent. It holds together, but is it true? Teilhard was convinced that the destiny of matter would be fulfilled but that individuals or civilizations could themselves fail to cooperate thus delaying that destiny. It is a basic tenet of

---

[8] Ken Keyes, Jr., *The Hundredth Monkey* (Vision Books, Coos Bay, Oregon, 1985) pp 11-17.
[9] *The Standard*, November/December, 1987, "Planet Earth Energized by Harmonic Convergence."

New Age thought that the only real sin is the refusal to live up to one's evolutionary duties and prepare for the inevitable future.

In this view it was not Satan or Adam and Eve who were the first sinners. Teilhard's ideas along this line are so comical that the reader will not believe me unless I quote: "[W]e may say it is the characteristic of minerals (as of so many other organisms that have become incurably fixed) to have chosen a road which closed them prematurely in upon themselves."[10]

The first sinners were rocks, rocks who chose the wrong road. The good rocks were those early minerals who lived up to their duties and eventually became megamolecules capable of forming the variable patterns required to make the breakthrough from pre-life to life. Then there were those sinful rocks who merely formed crystals capable of growing only according to a set pattern. We are urged not to look back to earlier patterns but instead to emulate those obedient forward-looking rocks by being open to the next step in our evolution.

Father Patrick O'Connell in his book, *Original Sin in the Light of Modern Science,* is right on the mark concerning Teilhard's ideas:

> In Father Teilhard's own country, France, prominent theologians, like Fr. Philip of the Trinity O.D.C., one of the Consultors of Vatican II, has analyzed his religious writings and pointed out the grave errors against the faith which they contain and prominent scientists like Professors Bounoure and Vernet of France have done the same for his scientific writings and have shown that he has no claim to be called a great scientist, or even to be called a scientist at all, but that he should rather be classified among the theosophists.[11]

---

[10]Pierre Teilhard de Chardin, *The Phenomenon of Man* (Harper Torchbook edition, Harper & Row, New York, 1965) pg 69.

[11]Rev. Patrick O'Connell, B.D., *Original Sin in the Light of Modern Science* (Lumen Christi Press, Houston, TX 1973) pg 46.

The founding of the Theosophical Society in 1875 was contemporaneous with the rise of liberal Protestantism and Catholic Modernism. Helena Petrovna Blavatsky and Colonel Henry Olcott lead the revival of what is called the Ancient Wisdom, an eclectic mix of Eastern mysticism, the Egyptian Mysteries, and Gnosticism as well as the writings of Plato, Plotinus and others. Evolution is a key doctrine. Dr. Douglas Baker, in his occult work, *Superconsciousness Through Meditation*, states:

> The first great postulate of Ancient Wisdom as set forth in *The Secret Doctrine* by Madame Blavatsky, is...the proposition that all things live. The tiniest atom is a sentinent [sic], living entity, as is the greatest galaxy in the heavens with its immense consciousness. Everything is alive: atoms are alive, minerals are alive, gemstones are alive.[12]

One of the most important Theosophist offshoots was Alice A. Bailey's Lucis Trust, founded in 1922. In that year her first book, *Initiation, Human and Solar,* was published by her Lucifer Publishing Company. It has since changed its name to the more covert "Lucis Publishing Company." Her works were dictated to her telepathically by one of the so called "Masters of Wisdom." It was these very ideas of the Theosophists which served as the seeds for the occultic, anti-semitic foundations of Nazism. Theosophists and Nazis both employ the swastika as their emblem. In Alice Bailey's teachings she wrote in 1939 about "the Jewish problem" and later, after the horrors of the Holocaust were made public, she still maintained that "[O]rthodox Judaism, with its deep-seated hatred, must slowly disappear."[13]

Constance Cumbey, in her excellent book about the New Age Movement, *Hidden Dangers of the Rainbow*, writes:

---

[12]Dr.Douglas Baker, *Superconsciousness Through Meditation* (Samuel Weiser, Inc., New York, NY, 1978) pg 30.

[13]Alice A. Bailey, *The Externalisation of the Hierarchy* (Lucis Publishing Co., New York, NY, 1982) pp 87, 543.

The writings of Alice Bailey, which have been followed meticulously by the New Age Movement, state that the new "messiah" will not be Jewish as the Jews have forfeited that privilege and that they must pass through the fires of purification in order to learn humility. (See *The Rays and the Initiations* by Alice A. Bailey. This particular passage regarding the New "Messiah" was written in 1949 when the entire world knew what had happened to Europe's Jewish population.) These teachings are also strongly opposed to "Zionism" and a possession of a homeland by the Jewish people. These teachings also state that what happened to the Jewish people in WW II was a result of their "bad national karma."[14]

The Alice Bailey writings call for a one world government, a one world leader called the "Christ", and a one world religion. It is not just the Jews who are a problem to them because any monotheistic belief which depends upon a transcendent God is hateful to them. The same teachings are equally anti-Christian and especially anti-Catholic. They speak of novel uses for atomic energy:

> The atomic bomb does not belong to the...nations who perfected it.... It belongs to the United Nations for use (or let us rather hope, simply for threatened use) when aggressive action . . . rears its ugly head. It does not essentially matter whether that aggression is the gesture of any particular nation or group of nations or whether it is generated by the political groups of any powerful religious organisation, such as the *Church of Rome, who as yet are unable to leave politics alone....*[15]

---

[14]Constance E. Cumbey, *The Hidden Dangers of the Rainbow: The New Age Movement and our Coming Age of Barbarism* (Huntington House, Inc., Shreveport, LA 1983) pg 115.

[15]Alice A. Bailey, *The Externalisation of the Hierarchy*, pg 548 (emphasis added).

Teilhard's Social Theories

If Teilhard had not spelled out his vision for mankind one might be tempted to speculate as to the nature of a society which is characterized by a single mind. As it is, Father Teilhard has made it very clear. In *Human Energy* he calls for a one world government as the only answer to world problems: "The age of nations has passed. Now, unless we wish to perish we must shake off our old prejudices and build the earth."[16]

Father Teilhard has not left much to the imagination as to the form he foresees for this one world government: "[N]o serious progress can be made...except under two conditions: the first that the proposed organization must be international *and in the end totalitarian*; and secondly that it must be conceived on a very large scale."[17]

The editor of *Human Energy* adds a footnote to this passage apologizing for Teilhard's unfortunate use of the word "totalitarian" saying that Teilhard meant to convey only a general notion of totality. In the *Future of Man* Teilhard writes: "[T]he modern totalitarian regimes, whatever their initial defects, are neither heresies nor biological regressions: They are in line with the essential trend of 'cosmic' movement.[18]

And who will rule in this glorious society? Obviously, Teilhard is not speaking of democracy or representative government, but of rule by an elite. The general population will not have a say in the future, rather:

> [T]he world of tomorrow will be born out of the elected
> group of those (arising from any direction and class, and

---

[16]Pierre Teilhard de Chardin, *Human Energy*, at 37.

[17]*Ibid.* at 134 (emphasis added).

[18]Pierre Teilhard de Chardin, *The Future of Man* (Harper & Row, New York, NY, 1969) pg 46.

confession in the human world) who will decide that there is something big waiting for us ahead, and give their life to reach it.[19]

This is not to contend that Teilhard envisioned a government that employs concentration camps and torture and murder, but what he does suggest can lead to little else. Teilhard appeals to something chillingly like the Nazi mentality of the 1930's or the ideas of present day euthanasia and abortion advocates. One wonders who would be the "useless eaters" in a Teilhardian society. He writes:

> The earth is a closed and limited surface. To what extent should it tolerate, racially or nationally, areas of lesser activity? More generally still, how should we judge the efforts we lavish on all kinds of hospitals on saving what is so often no more than life's rejects?
>
> To what extent should not the development of the strong (to the extent that we can define this quality) take precedence over the preservation of the weak? How can we reconcile, in a state of maximum efficiency, the care lavished on the wounded with the more urgent necessities of battle?[20]

Once again his editor, attempting to mitigate such outrageous statements, notes that "Teilhard's constant efforts both to encourage the weak and inspire the strong prove that he knew how to make this reconciliation." Although the above quotations are couched as questions, terms such as "maximum efficiency" and "lavish efforts" would seem to prejudice the answer, especially when Teilhard continues the above discussion using worried references to the increasing scarcity of natural resources and how they might best be allocated. Even with the Nazi Holocaust fresh in his

---

[19]Pierre Teilhard de Chardin, *Letters to Two Friends*, 1926-1952 (Meridian Books; World Publishing Co., New York, 1969) pg. 154.
[20]Pierre Teilhard de Chardin, *Human Energy*, at 132-33.

memory Teilhard's naivete is incredible. Once in a debate on the subject of *Science and Rationality*, "he shocked his opponent by refusing to permit even the appalling evidence of the experiments of the doctors of Dachau to modify his faith in the inevitability of human progress. 'Man,' he asserted, 'to become fully man, must have tried everything...'."[21]

Apparently, for Teilhard, evil is a necessary part of our evolution. But further, we cannot become "fully man" until we have committed every conceivable atrocity.

What are we to make of Teilhard's visions of a one world, elitist, totalitarian government? Where should we stand on his theology which speaks little of Christ, nearly nothing of Jesus and squares best with the teachings of occultists bent upon the destruction of Christianity? One can understand why he is the patron saint of New Agers, but then cultists and occultists have played at least a small part in every age, so why sound an alarm now? Because since his death Teilhard has become an increasingly fashionable figure within the church even though the condemnation of his works has never been revoked.

His writings have been translated into nearly every important language and the copies number in the many millions. His devotées include Assistant Secretary General of the United Nations, Robert Muller. Muller, a Roman Catholic described his "Five Teilhardian Enlightenments" in his book New Genesis. One of the best known "Teilhardians" is New York Governor, Mario Cuomo. Joseph Sobran, in the *National Right to Life News* (1/10/85) reported:

> Cuomo has spoken freely of his discovery of the writings of Teilhard de Chardin, the Jesuit theologian who fashioned a "scientific" yet mystical version of Catholicism for people who don't like Catholicism. Cuomo credits Teilhard's vision with making his own faith less rigid, more "humane."

---

[21]Mary Lukas and Ellen Lukas, *Teilhard*, at 237-38.

So he has apparently undergone some sort of inner conversion.[22]

Undoubtedly, many people are attracted to Teilhard because of his promise of inevitable progress for humanity. He offers a way out of our present predicament. It is apparent that many are grossly naive about certain of his political theories. Thomas M. King quotes Governor Cuomo's comments concerning Teilhard's political agenda in the March 30, 1985 issue of *America:*

> Perhaps the ideal is vague, but Teilhard never spelled out his politics. It is not easy to say what he would recommend in today's political world, but he would insist that we look beyond the differences that divide us and develop a sense of our common humanity. And he would also insist that such work is holy—for those who have the eyes to see.[23]

In his speech accepting the Democratic vice-presidential nomination in 1972, Sargent Shriver made reference to Teilhard. Teilhard has also been very well received by Marxists and even the Soviet Union has published a limited edition of the *Phenomenon of Man*, with numerous passages omitted.[24]

Fewer and fewer American Catholic publications are shy about quoting Teilhard glowingly. The Catholic Update turned its 1983 Christmas issue into a plug for New Age style activism. Writing about the New Creation: "We have only to believe," adds Teilhard de Chardin in *The Divine Milieu*, "then little by little, we shall see the universal horror unbend, and then smile upon us, and then take us in its more than human arms."[25]

---

[22]Joseph Sobran, National Right to Life News, January 10, 1985.

[23]Thomas M. King, America, March 30, 1985, pg 252.

[24]*Ibid.* at 252.

[25]Carol Luebering, *Catholic Update* (St. Anthony Messenger Press, Cincinnati, OH, 1983).

Whatever it may mean to one day find ourselves in the inhuman arms of a grinning universal horror, one thing is clear: the acceptance of the writings of Pierre Teilhard de Chardin is becoming a *fait accompli*. This is not to say that Teilhard has not composed occasional snippets that might be taken for orthodoxy. Certainly though, those are not the passages which endear him to the New Agers. On the other hand such passages provide his defenders with a few phrases with which to reassure Catholics who find him suspect. The writer of the article on Teilhard in the *New Catholic Encyclopedia* (1967) seems to bend over backwards in what is essentially a whitewash. The writer concedes that the Church has officially warned "against uncritical acceptance of his theories," but points out that the Church does not "question the value of his scientific work, or the righteousness of his intentions and the sincerity or fervor of his spiritual life." Of course, Teilhard is long dead and no one cares so much as a crumb about his science, his intentions or his sincerity. It is his *theories* that are embraced by the New Agers and questioned by the Church.

Teilhard is deadly. To such ideas as his, the door to the Church has always been barred. Barred to spiritualists, barred to witchcraft and the lie of the "god within." Today, as we face a world of extreme physical danger, the greater danger is spiritual and Teilhard has unbarred the door. The Christian needs discernment and increasingly; courage, remembering that:

> For there will come a time when they will not endure the sound doctrine; but having itching ears, will heap up to themselves teachers according to their own lusts. And they will turn away their hearing from the truth and turn aside rather to fables.
>
> (2 Timothy 4:3, 4)

5.

The New Age Mystic: Different Path, Same God?

That Eastern concepts have pervaded much of the West should be apparent to all but the most superficial observer. We have holistic health and holistic medicine. Transcendental Meditation and other mind control courses are multi-million dollar businesses. Due to the popularity of Shirley MacLaine's mystical books and her movie, *Out on a Limb*, Americans are becoming increasingly familiar with altered states of consciousness, past lives and reincarnation, and the contact of spirits through "trance channelers."

It comes, then, as no surprise, that the Church has felt a tug toward the East. There is a Catholic magazine called *Praying: Spirituality for Everyday Living*. The articles are, of course, concerned with prayer but unfortunately the emphasis is on New Age forms of prayer. One feature in the May-June, 1987 issue was a humorous piece, showing ten cartoons depicting various prayer types. Seven of the ten dealt with Oriental or occult techniques.[1]

---

[1]*Praying: Spirituality for Everyday Living*, May-June, 1987, "Favorite New Ways To Pray" by Kathleen Hightower.

Since the sixties there has occurred a surge of popularity in what is billed as the "revival of ancient Christian prayer" techniques. These techniques are so nearly identical to Eastern (or "pagan" in the West) meditative systems that the proponents of these methods generally feel compelled to make some apology in order to answer the objections of the uninitiated.

Typically, the argument develops one of two possible lines of defense. The more orthodox meditator will insist that what he is doing is in some way essentially different from Hindu meditation and is therefore "Catholic." The second sort is far more bold and even arrogant. He doesn't care that the only thing Christian in his prayer is the name he gives it. His belief is that all paths lead to God. But do they?

One Way to God?

Is the Christian path the only way to achieve eternal life with God? Or are other religions valid prescriptions for other peoples? Are Hinduism, Buddhism, Mormonism and African Religions valid paths to God? Let me be clear that when I speak of a Hindu, I mean one who practices orthodox Hindu religion. In the same way, a Mormon is one who follows the teachings of Joseph Smith and Brigham Young. If a person calls himself a Mormon, claims allegiance to Joseph Smith, but doesn't believe that God the Father is a flesh and blood man or that Jesus and Lucifer were brothers, then that person is not an orthodox Mormon. If instead, he ignores these doctrines, and begins to believe that Jesus Christ is the only begotten Son of God who came to die for his sins, but still calls himself a Mormon, then it would be arrogance for us to judge. The question I am raising concerns not this fellow in the middle but the true follower of other creeds.

A child in a religion class once defined "faith" as believing in something that you know isn't true. I have a friend who once repeated to me the old saw that the reason he believed in God was because "people need to believe in something greater than themselves." Some psychologists might agree that belief in God can be mentally healthful (although most would merely advise belief in oneself), but surely there can be only one valid reason for believing in *anything*, including belief in God. We believe in something because we think it true. This may seem obvious, but to a New Ager nothing is objectively true. What is truth for me may not be truth to him. He would say it is my truth, not his. You may recall that Jesus once had a discussion with this sort of person:

> Pilate therefore said to him, "Thou art then a king?" Jesus answered, "Thou sayest it; I am a king. This is why I was born, and why I have come into the world, to bear witness to the truth. Everyone who is of the truth hears my voice."
> Pilate said to him, "What is Truth?" (John 18:37-38).

Good question! If Hindus worship the same God as the Christian, then maybe they have something to teach us. But when Hinduism contradicts the Bible by teaching reincarnation and promising godhood for mankind, what shall we think? When Buddhism denies that Jesus is the one and only Christ, is it the Holy Spirit of God that inspires Buddhist doctrine? If God's Spirit is not behind the pagan religions then which spirit is?

Now someone might reasonably protest that there is much good to be learned from non-Christian religions and that we ought to be more open minded. True enough. That pagan religion has some good in it is not only observably true but one can go even further, saying that Satan himself has many "good" qualities. What we call evil started out as something good, but was then twisted and perverted. C.S. Lewis wrote:

> [E]vil is a parasite, not an original thing. The powers which enable evil to carry on are powers given it by goodness. All the things which enable a bad man to be effectively bad are

in themselves good things—resolution, cleverness, good looks, existence itself.[2]

The mere fact that a religion holds to an attractive ethical system is nothing. The New Agers like to say that all truth is God's truth. That's right. But whatever good baggage they have collected along the way—they got it from Him. If it upholds beauty instead of ugliness, kindness over cruelty, what does it prove? It may only show another good trait of the devil, that is, his intelligence. If one wants to lure another into some thing that may be harmful in the end, then paint a beautiful picture to trap the foolish. If a belief system is 99% true, but the remaining 1% is a fatal error then it will serve the devil perfectly. "For Satan himself disguises himself as an angel of light. It is no great thing then if his ministers disguise themselves as ministers of justice. But their end will be according to their works." (Corinthians 11:14,15).

About Himself, Jesus spoke, "I am the way, and the truth, and the life; no one comes to the Father but through me." (John 14:6)

St. Paul says, "Let him who takes pride, take pride in the Lord.... For other foundation no one can lay, but that which has been laid, which is Jesus Christ" (1 Corinthians 1:31;3:11). The Apostle goes much further in the same letter. After explaining the true way of salvation he continues by distinguishing the Eucharist from pagan sacrifices:

> [T]hey sacrifice to devils and not to God; and I would not have you become associates of devils. You cannot drink the cup of the Lord and the cup of devils; you cannot be partakers of the table of the Lord and the table of devils. (1 Corinthians 10:20-21)

Such strong words are not easy to take. It is easy to find individual Hindus who display more charity or patience than some

---

[2]C.S. Lewis, *Mere Christianity* (Macmillan Publishing Co., New York, 1979), pg. 35.

individual Christians. Many teachers are convinced that we have much to learn from the East, especially when Eastern meditation offers techniques and experiences which traditional Christianity apparently lacks. Does Oriental religion really offer value which Christianity does not?

Did the God who created the universe become a man and suffer a slow death by torture because Buddhism was already sufficient? Wouldn't some other less drastic means suffice? If a Hindu guru has the answer then Christianity is a cruel, inhuman hoax. Instead, we understand Christ's sacrifice and are confident that God has left nothing we need out of the Church He founded 2000 years ago.

Sadhana

Jesus offered no *guaranteed techniques* for those seeking experiences of God. The pattern Jesus gave stands out in sharp contrast to Eastern methods:

> When you pray, you shall not be like the hypocrites who love to pray standing in the synagogues and at the street corners in order that they be seen by men. Amen I say to you, they have received their reward. But when thou prayest, go to thy room, and closing thy door, pray to thy Father in secret; and thy Father, who sees in secret, will reward thee.
>
> But in praying, do not multiply words as the gentiles do; for they think that by saying a great deal, they will be heard. So do not be like them; for your Father knows what you need before you ask him. In this manner therefore shall you pray: "Our Father...."(Matthew 6:5-9)

To be a Catholic means, among other things, to have a hunger for God. The yearning for His presence is so strong, that Christians, even though aware of their complete unworthiness, can have no greater pleasure than to have fellowship with Him; to enjoy Him. It is this desire that makes many people receptive to teachers who promise to "teach us to pray."

Let's explore the writings of one of these teachers to illustrate what has been passing for "spirituality" in the Church in recent years. I have not singled out this author/lecturer because he is alone in what he teaches or because he is the most "Eastern." He is merely representative.

Father Anthony de Mello was a Jesuit from India. An internationally noted speaker until his sudden death in 1987, he led workshops on the subject of Eastern and Western prayer experiences and wrote the "How to do it" book: *Sadhana: a Way to God*. Subtitled "Christian Exercises in Eastern Form," Sadhana is published in the U.S. by The Institute of Jesuit Sources, St. Louis, Missouri. The cover of the book shows Jesus upon the cross. At his feet sits a meditating figure, legs crossed in the traditional lotus position.

Sadhana's Foreword to the North American Edition suggests to the reader that trendy Catholics ought to jump onto the meditation bandwagon or risk being left behind. After all, it must be good, considering how many important people are helping to drag this pagan idol into the church.

The 700,000 American practitioners of Transcendental Meditation (TM) are cited approvingly as one indication of the growing interest in Oriental religions and techniques for achieving the contemplative (read "altered") state of mind. It says that TM can be either Christian or Zen Buddhist prayer. Continuing, the foreword cites Father William Johnston from his book, *The Still Point: Reflections on Zen and Christian Mysticism:*

> [N]ot only Zen but all forms of Buddhism are going to make an enormous impact on the Christianity of the coming century.... [T]here is every likelihood that the future will see the rise of an Oriental Christianity in which the role

of Buddhism will be incalculably profound. Indeed this process has already begun.[3]

Before giving instructions de Mello gives two caveats. First, he explains that the reader will not master the material by reading it. It is necessary to "experience" the things taught. Secondly, he gives the first of several veiled warnings about possible dangers that could arise from the practice of his exercises.

The author takes the seeker through a number of exercises beginning simply enough with the preparatory stage of stillness:

> Close your eyes once again. Get in touch with sensations...of your body.... You will gradually feel a certain stillness in your body. Do not explicitly rest in the stillness.
> I repeat, do not explicitly rest in the stillness.... If you do so, you run the danger of inducing a mild trance.... [4]

Soon though, de Mello allows that if the stillness overpowers you, let go and surrender to it. Enjoy! Soon the novice learns that only through achieving altered states of consciousness is he able to understand reality. By the time the seeker reaches exercise number three, he has already learned reluctance to answer foolish questions about his experience. De Mello writes:

> What is the benefit of all this...? The only reply I shall give you for now is: Don't ask questions.
> You will also experience a disinclination to answer the questions, even seemingly practical questions, of others on these matters.... [T]he only worthy answer to them is, "Open your eyes and see for yourself."[5]

[3] Anthony de Mello, *Sadhana: a Way to God, Christian Exercises in Eastern Form* (The Institute of Jesuit Sources, St. Louis, 1978) pg x.
[4] *Ibid.* at 14, 15.
[5] *Ibid.* at 16.

Before the novice can progress very far into the depths of the mind he must become the mind's master. A key to mind control is correct body posture. As in the traditional Hindu meditation the most effective position is with the back and head erect. Fr. de Mello writes:

> The ideal posture for this is the lotus posture that students of yoga are taught: legs intertwined with feet resting upon opposite thighs and spine erect. I am told that people who manage to attain this posture have such little difficulty with distractions that they actually have trouble thinking and getting their thinking mind to function at all.[6]

Once the mind and the posture are right it is time for breathing exercises. The novice is to concentrate on the air flowing through the nostrils; its temperature, its volume. He is to keep his awareness on the breath for only ten to fifteen minutes. De Mello cautions against using this exercise for extended periods, at least not without a competent "guide." He mentions possible hallucinations from the practice, and warns that it may dredge up unspecified "material" from the meditator's unconscious which he may find uncontrollable. The dangers are real, not only spiritually but mentally as well. For a more forthright explanation of the "Perils of the Path" here are a few excerpts from the (non-Christian) book by Eknath Easwaran, *Meditation: Commonsense Directions For an Uncommon Life*:

> Please do not, in a burst of enthusiasm, increase your meditation to an hour or longer, because such a practice exposes you to dangers.
> What dangers?...a few [people] have an inborn capacity to plunge deeply inward. And once you break through the surface level, you are in an uncharted world. It is like a desert, but instead of sand there are latent

---

[6]*Ibid.* at 20.

psychological tendencies, terribly powerful forces. There you stand in that vast desert without a compass. You have tapped forces before you are prepared to handle them, and your daily life can be adversely affected by them.

You may see lights, perhaps brilliant ones, or hear sounds.

Entering deeper consciousness is like descending into a cave. There are bewitching experiences, and there can also be awesome, even disorienting ones.

One last warning: please do not try to connect the passage to a physiological function, such as heartbeat or breathing rhythm. Such a connection may seem helpful initially, but it can cause serious problems later. Trying to synchronize your mantram with physiological processes, such as heartbeat or breathing, also divides your attention. No harm will result if this happens by itself, but do not try to make the connection. Actually, it can be quite hazardous to interfere with vital functions that are already operating smoothly without our conscious intervention.[7]

What is being implied here? That one can kill himself doing Yoga? Understandably, modern writers hoping to promote the practice are loathe to dwell on the subject, but ancient Yoga texts are more forthright. The writer of the *Hatha Yoga Pradipika* warns "the breath is controlled by slow degrees, otherwise [by being hasty or using too much force] it *kills the practicer himself.*"[8]

It is impossible to read very much about meditation without receiving such warnings. Even openly Luciferic publications contain dark admonishments against "opening doors on to the astral plane which the student may have difficulty in closing."[9]

---

[7]Eknath Easwaran, *Meditation: Commonsense Directions for an Uncommon Life* (Nilgiri Press, Petaluma, CA, 1978) pg 43, 53, 54, 71.

[8]*Hatha Yoga Pradipika*, at 15 (emphasis added).

[9]Alice A. Bailey, *Externalisation of the Hierarchy* (Lucis Publishing Co., New York, NY, 1982) pg 18.

Hopefully, these red flags may tend to warn off some potential seekers. The authors of meditation guides advise exercising extreme caution unless accompanied by a "competent guide." Such books would perform a more valuable service if they plainly warned against monkeying around with these practices at all.

In *Sadhana* we are told that, "Our Hindu masters in India have a saying: One thorn is removed by another. By this they mean that you will be wise to use one thought to rid yourself of all the other thoughts.... The mind must have something to occupy it...an ejaculation that you keep repeating ceaselessly to prevent the mind from wandering.... [O]ne thorn is just as good as another."[10] Later though, de Mello adds that when engaged in group chanting the Sanskrit word OM is a great help. Also helpful is the regular striking of "a pleasant sounding gong.[11]

The mantra has a place in most of the popular eastern oriented systems. Some writers emphasize it more than others. Some, trying to seem less pagan will advise using it only as often as needed to drive out distractions. For some meditators this means constant repetition, while for more adept "contemplatives" the altered state of mind is maintained with minimal use of the mantra.

The mantra may be any sound, although certain sounds are considered more effective for particular purposes. OM is considered especially powerful. While it may or may not have meaning for the meditator, the mantra should consist of a single word. Whole sentences or scripture verses—which incidentally might be contemplated to very worthwhile ends—are not usually advised because they might provoke thoughts. The Catholic seeker is often advised to use a "Christian" mantra such as:

Jesus...Jesus...Jesus...Jesus...Jesus...Jesus...Jesus
...Jesus...Jesus...Jesus...Jesus...Jesus...Jesus...Jesus...
Jesus...Jesus...Jesus...Jesus...Jesus...Jesus...Jesus...

---

[10]Anthony de Mello, *Sadhana*, at 28-29.
[11]*Ibid.* at 45.

It would seem that the thrust is to "baptize" non-Christian behavior with sacred trappings in order to make them acceptable to Christians. Occult practices cannot be so sanctified, but rather the Holy Name is profaned instead. Also, how many times can one repeat thoughtlessly any single word without recalling the command of Jesus quoted above when he forbade praying with vain repetitions.

It is reminiscent of the triumph of Elijah over the Prophets of Baal (1 Kings 18). Elijah challenged the Baal worshippers, pitting the God of Israel against the pagan god. As the heathen called down fire from heaven they repeated endlessly from morning till noon: "O Baal, Hear us! O Baal, Hear us! O Baal!" etc..... Well, they worked up quite a lather dancing and chanting and slashing themselves with swords but they got nothing but taunts from Elijah for their efforts. Contrast this with Elijah's brief prayer:

> "Lord, God of Abraham, and Isaac, and Israel, show us this day that thou art the God of Israel, and I thy servant, and that according to thy commandment I have done all these things. Hear me, O Lord, Hear me: that this people may learn, that thou art the Lord God, and that thou hast turned their heart again."
>
> Then the fire of the Lord fell.   (1 Kings 18:36-38)

Now that's effective prayer! This is not to say that repeating a mantra is not effective at inducing the thoughtless state of mind. In fact, this is the chief defense made by the typical Christian guru against charges of "multiplying words as the gentiles do." He answers that the "prayer word" is used to facilitate union with the Lord. In other words, it works, so how can it be "vain?"[12]

---

[12]M. Basil Pennington, *Centering Prayer*, at 200.

What is the Difference Anyway?

It is important to further distinguish between occult meditation, which is the foundation of all New Age beliefs, and Christian
meditation which is basic to true spiritual growth. First, what New
Agers call meditation is nothing like Christian *meditation*. *Meditative* (or discursive) prayer, for the Christian, consists of a rational
examination of God's truths, commands, mysteries or events from
Holy Scripture. Notice how the psalmist uses meditation:

> I will *meditate* on your precepts, and consider your ways.

> Make me understand the ways of your precepts, and I will
> *meditate* on your wondrous deeds.

> I have more understanding than all my teachers when your
> decrees are my *meditation*.   (Psalm 119:15,27,99)

> How I love your law, O LORD! It is my *meditation* all the
> day. (Psalm 119:97)

> Happy the man who...delights in the law of the LORD and
> *meditates* on his law day and night. (Psalm 1:1,2)

Beyond meditative prayer, there is the genuine mystical experience of *contemplation*. Contemplation is the absorption of the
soul into a partial vision of God. While various Catholic traditions
employ differing practices to prepare for contemplation, the
Divine vision is a gift God gives as He wills. Neither human reason
nor the mindless techniques of bearded gurus have power to
produce visions of God. Yet here, at the level of such a towering
gift, Satan best earns his title, the "ape of God." The practice of
contemplation is dangerous because, as a gift independent of
reason, the impact is upon the senses and the emotions—fertile
ground for counterfeiting by the devil. The Catholic tradition is one
of great caution and the need for proper spiritual direction and the
discernment of a good director. Otherwise, we are easily fooled by
the fraudulent offerings of spiritual quacks in their imitation of
contemplation.

Unlike occult meditation, whose goal is an opened and emptied mind, Christian prayer has God as its object. The object (or mantra) of occult meditation is a mere mental device, which when properly employed, results in an empty and open receptacle. This emptying and inversion into self gazes at nothing and waits for what it doesn't know. This should be contrasted with the Christian at prayer: he knows his object and turns toward God, not self. It is not the glory of the god within, but the magnificent goodness of the transcendent God which strikes most palpably. The meditator is intent upon God and His Word; not as a means to an end, but as the end itself.

Not only is Christian meditation different in its method, it is different in its result. Occult meditation strives toward realization of oneness with the universe or ultimate reality or whatever it calls its god. The Christian too, wants union with God; that is, to have God's mind, His heart, and His presence, but not identification with Him. True, our destiny is to be glorified and "conformed to the image of His Son" (Romans 8:29-30), but this is not equivalence or identity with God. We shall have His spiritual nature and shall be with Him. How can any Christian wish for more? The perfect picture of eternity is given us in Revelation:

> Behold the dwelling of God with men, and He will dwell with them. And they will be His people and God himself will be with them as their God. And God will wipe away every tear from their eyes. And death shall be no more; neither shall there be mourning, nor crying, nor pain any more, for the former things have passed away.   (Revelation 21:3-4)

It is impossible to reconcile these eastern teachings and practices with either the Bible or the traditions of the Church. Tradition consists of the teachings handed down through time as developed by the whole body of Christ. Of course, the absolute truths of Scripture never change but tradition is steadily enriched. What is so amazing is that these gurus feel it is their position, even their duty, to singlehandedly enrich the tradition. In this way, their definition of tradition justifies the eastern embellishments. One popular teacher writes:

> This gift of life has been handed on through the ensuing centuries, sixteen or so, till it has come down to us today. In our own time it has been gifted with a new name, Centering Prayer, and a new packaging, the impress of our hands as we pass it on to other, younger eager minds and hearts. They too, as they receive it, mold it and, we hope, will pass it on in a fruitful and life giving way.... I have not separated East from West, for, as I have indicated, the Jesus Prayer in its purest form is but another expression of the same tradition springing from the same source.[13]

Unfortunately, the legitimate development of tradition is used as an excuse for meddling beyond the limits of tradition and into areas where Scripture has warned us away.

Another aid to successful meditation that Fr. de Mello suggests is to have the correct location for meditation. It is a common occult/eastern belief that places have their own vibrations. Good "vibes" enhance meditations and bad "vibes" inhibit. He recommends:

> [Y]ou make your contemplation each time in the same place, the same corner, a corner or a room that is reserved for this purpose only.... [I]t helps to pray in 'sacred' places that have been sanctified by the frequent practice of contemplation.[14]

---

[13] *Ibid.* at 22.
[14] Anthony de Mello, *Sadhana* at 55.

Father Basil Pennington, the father of modern "centering prayer" and admirer of Anthony de Mello adds to the "vibes" discussion:

> We in the West are not so sensitively aware of vibrations. Yet they inevitably take their toll on us. A room that has been very full of busy activity or loud, hard music carries its charge long after. It is well to be aware of this when we have a choice of places to meditate.[15]

This concept of vibrations is purely an eastern/occult idea; it is not of Christian origin. In comparing the way of Sadhana to the techniques of occultist meditation one must look very hard to find any differences. Most methods will advise reserving a room (or at least a corner) for meditation. It is to be used for no other purpose. Gradually the room or corner becomes "sacred." Some say it helps to have a picture of your favorite mystic hanging on the wall somewhere.[16]

Visualization and Spirit Guides

When I was nineteen years old I had the unfortunate experience of spending some time with a fellow who introduced me to the concept of visualization. Bob was ten years older than my friends and me. When he moved into our small town and opened up what was called a "head shop," many local teens, including myself, were drawn to this peculiar stranger. He was different from most other 30 year olds and seemed to enjoy our "hanging out" at his shop as well as joining us at our weekend parties. Bob's hair was long and over his ears, as was common at the time, a fact which made it all the more eerie when I saw an oil portrait of him in his

[15]M. Basil Pennington, O.C.S.O., *Centering Prayer: Renewing an Ancient Christian Prayer Form* (Doubleday & Co., Garden City, NY, 1980) pg 4.
[16]Eknath Easwaran, *Meditation* at 45.

home. His hair was pulled back in this painting and I remember wondering to myself why anyone would want to portray themselves with pointed ears like the devil.

One weekend evening, my friends and I were out talking with Bob in a quiet park. Only those in our small group were present and Bob chose that night to reveal to us that he was a witch. He explained (and demonstrated) to us his use of hypnosis, an important part of his "craft." Most important though and the real source of his power, he told us, was the technique of visualization.

"I killed a man once," he said. Everyone squirmed at his statement but not one of us said a word in the darkness. Bob sensed our discomfort and explained:

> He was very bad and deserved to die. I would never use my power for evil purposes. The way I did it was like this: I sat on the floor in my room with my feet facing this guy's house. Then I went into a trance and began to visualize, over and over, this man having his brains beaten out with a hammer. I just kept that picture happening in my mind again and again.
>
> That night while driving, he lost control of his car on a curve. He was thrown out and had his skull crushed on the pavement.

It was a sobering and disquieting story to hear. I and most of my friends stayed away from Bob after that. That brief association with this self-proclaimed witch still makes me shudder and I thank God for pulling me away from him even at a time when God did not seem so important in my life.

It was this story which came back to my mind as I began to study the New Age movement. Without any doubt visualization is the foundation and basis for witchcraft, so-called "mind powers" and pagan shamanism. It is found in African and Native American religion in the practice of the witch doctor or medicine man.

Visualization is the attempt to manipulate the physical world or contact the spirit world by use of the imagination. Tony de Mello, in *Sadhana*, teaches visualization as a technique for contacting Jesus:

> Imagine you see Jesus sitting close to you....
> Now speak to Jesus.... If no one is around, speak out in a soft voice.
> Listen to what Jesus says to you in reply...or what you imagine him to say.
> People sometimes ask me how they can meet the Risen Lord in their lives. I know of no better way to suggest to them than this one.[17]

In another exercise, he asks the meditator to pick a symbol for God. It may be anything, a flower or a star (since the symbol doesn't matter, presumably even a golden calf or a Swastika would do):

> Having chosen your symbol, stand reverently in front of it.... Say something to it...
> Now imagine that it speaks back to you.... What does it say?[18]

Getting the chance to personally meet Jesus (short of heaven) would seem to be appealing but such efforts are not in accord with Scripture. Regarding this issue of seeing Jesus, compare the above exercises with an epistle penned by St. Peter:

> Him, though you have not seen, you love. In him, though you do not see him, yet believing, you exult with a joy unspeakable and triumphant; receiving, as the final issue of your faith, the salvation of your souls. (1 Peter 1:8,9).

What is going on when the Christian goes into the reaches of the mind to get in touch with God? What harm can come from it and besides, if the vision helps then doesn't that prove the validity of the experience? It should be plain that the *fact* of the experience

---

[17]Anthony de Mello, *Sadhana*, at 72-73.
[18]*Ibid.* at 80.

is no indicator of its source. Just because the image speaks is no evidence that God has been contacted. Anyone who finds themselves able to "call up" God is either being fooled by his own imagination or worse, is in touch with a deceiving spirit.

At other points Fr. de Mello directs the reader to visualize a meeting with an old hermit, or conversing with statues and even one sick exercise where you see your own cold corpse turning blue and rotting as the decomposed flesh falls away.[19] Contrast these techniques with the sort of meditation defined in the Spiritual Exercises of Saint Ignatius (from which de Mello claims to draw much inspiration):

> Meditation consists in calling to mind some dogmatic or moral truth and reflecting on or discussing this truth according to each one's capacity, so as to move the will and produce in us amendment.[20]

Similarities between the Ignatian exercises and *Sadhana* are few. While St. Ignatius' exercises do sometimes require the picturing of biblical scenes upon which the student meditates, these are exercises of the thinking mind. There is no altered state of consciousness by which the meditator empties himself and invites the "spirit" to speak to him.

Sadhana is clearly a different beast; one that correlates well with eastern/occult sources and hardly at all with the Christian tradition. Some of these exercises are merely strange, others are probably harmless, but many (such as recorded here) move into realms through which no human can safely travel.

---

[19] Anthony de Mello, Sadhana, at 81, 92.
[20] *Spiritual Exercises of St. Ignatius* (Frederick Pustet & Co., New York, 1914) pg 54.

Rewriting the Scriptures

Another recently popular technique is Ira Progoff's *Intensive Journal* method. In workshops, retreats and in tape series Catholics and others are taught that keeping the journal will enhance their spirituality. Of course there is nothing wrong with recording and reflecting upon insights gained in one's spiritual life. The question is more about which religious insights will be reflected upon and from what source they will be gained. The assumption seems to be that our Scriptures are no longer relevant and that we can do better rewriting them based on our own life experiences and meditations.

Dr. Ira Progoff, psychotherapist, professor and author, studied with psychiatrist/occultist C.G. Jung and afterward with Zen master D.T. Suzuki. He clearly presents his journaling method in his book *At a Journal Workshop*. The back dust jacket should be quite inviting for Roman Catholics. Among the glowing reviews is one by a Catholic university professor and another by a priest who calls Progoff's workshop "the greatest single breakthrough in my spiritual life.... I would like to see every pastoral person get a chance to experience this."[21]

Part of the journaling experience is called Twilight Imaging, done in what Progoff calls an "intermediate state of consciousness" somewhere between sleep and waking. In this altered state we "behold" inward "perceptions" which present themselves unasked for.[22] In another lesson the image gets clearer with an exercise which is wholly occult and nearly indistinguishable from the spirit guides of the Silva Mind Control method.

The "Inner Wisdom Dialogue" begins with the student entering the meditative state. A being chosen by the student arrives to impart the inner wisdom (although an unexpected figure may appear instead). Progoff narrates:

---

[21]Ira Progoff, *At a Journal Workshop* (Dialogue House Library, New York, 1975) Dust jacket.
[22]*Ibid.* at 77-79.

We let our thoughts come to rest. Our breathing is slow. It becomes slower, softer. We are still.

In the stillness we feel the presence of this person, this wisdom figure, this being.

They speak to us.

We speak and we are spoken to. And we let it be written through our pen.[23]

As usual, the communications are automatically assumed to be valuable. In time, the meditator can expect to make contact with a number of these spirit guides. Add to this the common demonic device of dictating written material through a medium and the whole picture should be clear enough to warn off even the half-asleep Christian. Incredible as it may seem though, "thousands of priests, nuns and lay people, as well as official Catholic 'spiritual renewal' institutions are enthusiastically embracing this method."[24] I have copies of the annual schedule for the Intensive Journal workshops and retreats. Recent years show *dozens* of Catholic retreat houses and colleges sponsoring the method each year.

One might think some of the advice as doled out by the visualized images would be questioned, but this is never given any serious thought. The opposite sentiment is actually the rule because the experience is always considered self-authenticating. One writer explained why only good can come to those who open themselves up to this experiential religion. Although the excerpt below refers to "centering prayer," the author has admitted that the prayer experience produces the desire for closer contact with non-Christian practice:[25]

[W]e need have no fear of the deceptions of the Evil One, because he cannot touch us at that level of our being. He

---

[23]*Ibid.* at 281-84.

[24]Ralph Martin, *A Crisis of Truth* (Servant Books, Ann Arbor, MI, 1982) pg 63.

[25]M. Basil Pennington, *America*, February 28, 1987, pg 171.

> can only affect those images and feelings that are in-
> fluenced through the body. He cannot himself penetrate
> into our spiritual being. There is a danger...in active
> prayer, in which we are using our imagination and feelings,
> for he can influence these. But in Centering Prayer we
> ignore these faculties...so the Evil One cannot touch it. We
> are engaged at a level that the Lord has made his own....
> We are out of the Devil's reach. Only God can penetrate
> this level of our being. So we are completely safe....[26]

Thus everything is turned upside down. The danger is in our
bedtime prayers because there we pray under the influence of our
thinking minds and tired bodies. But safety is in the brainless
opening of an empty mind with the solemn assurance that Satan
cannot function in the spirit realm. Is Satan really unable to
"penetrate our spiritual being?" If we mean "Can he control our
intellect and will?, then no. Even the demoniacs of the New Testament were not acting out their own will but rather that of the
possessing demon. But that is no comfort when the victim's own
will has voluntarily opened the door to the spirits. The simple fact
that these practices appear to grease the skids for more advanced
occult practices should warn us from taking even the first step. We
must remember with whom we are dealing. It is St. Paul who
reminds us that the spiritual realm is the devil's natural element:

> For our wrestling is not against flesh and blood, but against
> the Principalities and Powers, against the world-rulers of
> this darkness, against the spiritual forces of wickedness on
> high.
>
> (Ephesians 6:12)

May God keep safe the unwary souls who venture there.

---

[26]M. Basil Pennington, *Centering Prayer* at 191-92.

6.

WomanChurch, Witchcraft, and the Goddess

Fr. Matthew Fox

One of the most enigmatic spectacles in modern Catholic America is the popularity of Dominican priest Father Matthew Fox. His books *Whee! We, wee* and *On Becoming a Musical, Mystical Bear* and *Original Blessing* (and others) can be found on the shelves of most Catholic as well as occultic bookstores. As any Catholic knows and as the Church teaches, sin is inherited from Adam and is only removed through Christ's redemption.[1] The Scripture too, is in exact agreement: "For just as by the disobedience of the one man the many were constituted sinners, so also by the obedience of the one the many will be constituted just" (Romans 5:19).

In *Original Blessing*, Fox denies the traditional doctrine of original sin. He says we do not enter existence as sinful creatures:

---

[1]Ludwig Ott, *Fundamentals of Catholic Dogma* (Tan Books, Rockford, IL 1974) pg 108.

"We burst into the world as 'Original Blessings.'" The only sin Fox recognizes is the sin of dualism; i.e., of seeing people and things as being separate from one another. The only sin is the refusal to see all as one.[2]

His brand of religion is aptly called "Creation-Centered Spirituality." Creation-Centered Spirituality is focused not on God the Creator, but on god the creation. Father Fox is calling for Catholics to be in the leadership of the new spiritual age.

In her book *A Planned Deception*, Constance Cumbey wrote a chapter entitled "The Incredible Heresies of Father Matthew Fox." She related her experience of hearing Matthew Fox address parish leaders in a talk sponsored by the Liturgy Committee of the Archdiocese of Detroit:

> He shamelessly committed public blasphemy against the Holy Spirit, by telling an impressionable audience well under the spell of his hypnotic powers that the Holy Spirit was demanding they adopt wicca (witchcraft), shamanism, and goddess worship. Hundreds of well dressed parish leaders and nuns listened to him in trance-like rapture. They appeared to adore Matthew Fox! One distinguished looking CCD teacher proudly told me that he had taught St. Thomas Aquinas and St. Augustine for 30 years. "That was" he said "a waste of time. I wish I had been teaching Father Matthew Fox!"[3]

As with all orthodox New Agers, Fox insists that sin consists in the failure to embrace the New Age, the age of Aquarius. He warns in *Whee! We, wee All the Way Home...A Guide to a Sensual, Prophetic Spirituality*:

---

[2]Matthew Fox, *Original Blessing: A Primer in Creation Spirituality*, (Bear & Company, Inc., Santa Fe, NM, 1983) pg 47, 49.
[3]Constance Cumbey, *A Planned Deception: The Staging of a New Age Messiah*, (Pointe Publishers, Inc., East Detroit, MI 1985) pg 133.

One tradition that offers us a glimpse into our own futures ... is the astrological tradition.

In particular, Jung subscribes to the way of seeing human history in 2000-year stages corresponding to the Age of the Bull (4000-2000 B.C.), a symbol of primitive instinctual civilizations and represented by Cretan religion; the Age of the Ram (2000 B.C.-1 A.D), characterized by the religions of the Jews and the emergence of conscience and awareness of evil wherein religion sacrificed rams; the Age of Pisces, the fishes, (1 A.D.-1997 A.D.), dominated religiously by the figure of Christ....

There is an extremely important Caveat and danger sign that looms on our journey. That is the warning not to look back.... If you recall, when Moses came down from his experience with God on the mountain top, he was so infuriated by what he saw the Israelites doing that he broke the commandment tablets. What were they doing? They were whoring after the past gods! They were worshipping the religion of the previous age, the Age of the Bull. They refused to face the new spiritual consciousness that Moses ushered in, that of the Age of the Ram.

So we, too, on the verge of breaking into a new spiritual age, need to beware of the Gods of the past.... We have a clear lesson from the Israelites: to look back piningly is to commit idolatry.[4]

What delusion is it that allows Catholics to believe teaching which insists that to remain within traditional, biblical Christianity is idolatry; that it is "whoring after past gods?" It seems impossible that anyone could be so deceived, but in his second letter to the Thessalonians, St. Paul wrote of how those who were headed for destruction would not turn aside from their chosen course:

---

[4]Matthew Fox, O.P., *Whee! We, wee All the Way Home.... A Guide to a Sensual, Prophetic Spirituality* (Bear & Company, Inc., Santa Fe, NM, 1981) pp 30, 242.

> For they have not the love of truth that they might be
> saved. Therefore God sends them a misleading influence
> that they may believe falsehood, that all may be judged who
> have not believed the truth, but have preferred wicked-
> ness.   (2 Thessalonians 2:10-12)

Whereas Pierre Teilhard de Chardin bridges the gap between East and West, Matthew Fox champions the paganism of the West. Like Teilhard, he worships matter as his God, but Fox repudiates Teilhard for his belief in self-denial and renunciation of pleasure seeking.[5] He believes that "enough evils and crosses exist in our lives without making up new ones."[6] Fox is perhaps the American Church's most enthusiastic cheerleader for hedonism or what he calls "ecstasy."

In the New Age movement drugs can be more than just a way to have fun and pass the time until "the Christ" comes. Drugs can play an important role in altering consciousness. Whether it is the LSD popularized in the 60's or the peyote of the Indian sorcerer in the Carlos Casteñada books, the use of drugs serves as a shortcut to mystical experience. The same occult meditative states that normally require extended practice to achieve are effortlessly attained through drug use. The same experiences and even the spirits encountered are common to either method. In fairness, most genuine gurus will snub the drug user's "training wheels" as an expedient which does not ultimately lead to the very highest (or lowest?) states.

In Fox's book, *On Becoming a Musical, Mystical Bear*, he has written that while "excess" drug use is not wise, "intelligent use of drugs" is unquestionably an aid to prayer. Its value, says Fox, is in

---

[5]*Ibid.*, pp 217-18.
[6]Matthew Fox, "Self denial can make you selfish," *U.S. Catholic*, February 1978, pg 37.

opening up one's awareness and also as a temporary escape from the worries of the everyday world. He maintains that "drugs can democratize spirituality, which has for so long been imagined to be in the hands and hearts of the wealthy, leisurely classes."[7]

Before looking further into Fox's paganism, it is worth examining his view of Jesus. In *Original Blessing*, Father Fox rates numerous historical figures on their *creation-centeredness*. On a scale of one to five Jesus gets a "five," but (as in the theology of Teilhard) Jesus really has no place at all except as an example of a wise man among other wise men and women.[8] He says Jesus *"was always looking for wisdom in order to grow in wisdom"* and refers to Jesus as *"weak and imperfect."*[9] One has to ask: Where is Father Fox getting this picture of Christ? In his latest book, *The Coming of the Cosmic Christ*, Fox laments Jesus' "cruel and premature death."[10] He says, "no one can ever bring back the time that Jesus lost and will never live out. His was truly an untimely death if ever there was one."[11]

Father Fox seems not to have heard that Jesus is alive after having spent just three days in the grave; seems not to understand the very reason Jesus was born. Rejecting the truth that Jesus came to die for man's sins he paints a picture not of Jesus resigning Himself to His Father's will but as trying to escape His sacrifice. Speaking of Jesus facing the crucifixion he says, "How thoroughly he rejects it, flies from it, desires it prevented. 'Let this cup pass from me.' Yet he fails and the crucifiers have their way."[12] It is

[7]Matthew Fox, *On Becoming a Musical, Mystical Bear: Spirituality American Style* (Paulist Press, New York, N.Y. 1976) pp 125-27.

[8]Matthew Fox, *Original Blessing,* pg 307.

[9]*Ibid.*, at 122.

[10]Matthew Fox, *The Coming of the Cosmic Christ* (Harper & Row, San Francisco, 1988) pg 71.

[11]*Ibid.* at 140.

[12]Matthew Fox, O.P., *Whee! We, wee...*, pg 93.

difficult to see how such an uninspiring Jesus could be the same person who created the universe. But He is, as St Paul tells us,

> the image of the invisible God, the firstborn of every creature. For in Him were created all things in the heavens and on the earth, things visible and things invisible, whether Thrones, or Dominations, or Principalities, or Powers. All things have been created through and unto Him. and He is before all creatures, and in Him all things hold together. (Colossians 1:15-17).

Matthew Fox also sees the miracles of the Bible through the perspective of his creation spirituality. Our traditional fall/redemption theology accepts miracles as an intervention by the supernatural into the natural order of things. Fox sees a naturalistic explanation in Christ's miracle of the loaves and the fishes: "[T]he real miracle that Jesus wrought was not a quantitative magic trick of turning five loaves and two fishes into thousands. The true miracle was that Jesus got people to let go, to share with one another."[13]

In *A Spirituality Named Compassion*, Fox insists that Jesus was not good because he was God, but instead was divine because he was good. This denies the objective divinity of Jesus. Specifically, he writes: "Jesus is not so much compassionate because he is divine as he is divine because he is compassionate. And did he...not teach others that they too were...divine because they are compassionate?[14]

At best he considers Jesus not as the God who created the universe, but as a sort of drum major out in front of the parade we should all be in. His lip service to Jesus as the most "creation-centered" human ever to live is mere pandering. One wonders why

---

[13]Matthew Fox, *Original Blessing*, pg 170.
[14]Matthew Fox, *A Spirituality Named Compassion and the Healing of the Global Village, Humpty Dumpty and Us* (Winston Press, Inc., Minneapolis, MN 1979) pg 34.

he wastes good ink on Him. If Matthew Fox has any historical reference point it is in the person of the 14th century German mystic, Meister Eckhart.

Eckhart was born around 1260 A.D. entering the Dominican order while a youth. A popular speaker, his pantheistic ideas strongly identified God with his creation. Eckhart has been hailed as a forerunner to Theosophists, Nazis and Pantheists. Hindus regard him as a "kindred spirit."[15] He felt that a God "out there" was unfathomable. Evelyn Underhill, in her book *The Mystics of the Church*, wrote that Eckhart had

> a tendency to exile God from His creation; and led him to set up a sharp distinction between the Absolute and unconditioned Godhead, "unknown and never to be known," and the God of religious experience. This separation is fundamental to Eckhart's thought....
>
> [T]his leaning to transcendental speculation, land[ed] him at last in a monism which...can hardly be reconciled with Christianity.[16]

Eckhart saw a unity between God and man and he tended to see Jesus as the first human to realize that unity. Many of his ideas can be taken in more than one sense. The result is that one meaning may be insightful while the second meaning is solidly heretical. In one of his sermons he said, "If God's being is my being, then God's existence must be my existence and His essence my essence...." In another he said, "...the Holy Spirit receives his being...from me as from God."[17]

It was his radical ideas combined with his popularity that eventually brought him into conflict with the local authorities. Near

---

[15]James M. Clark, *Meister Eckhart* (Thomas Nelson and Sons, London,1957) pg vi.

[16]Evelyn Underhill, *The Mystics of the Church* (Schocken Books, New York, NY 1971) pg 134.

[17]James M. Clark, *Meister Eckhart*, pp 187, 141.

the end of his life in 1326, he was cited for heresy by a hostile tribunal in his native Germany. Eckhart appealed to the pope for an unbiased hearing. He agreed to repudiate any teachings which were found to be heretical, but died before his case was decided.

In 1329, the year after his death, 17 of his propositions were condemned as heretical in the bull (*In Agro Dominico*) of Pope John XII. It was declared that he had been deceived "by the father of lies who often appears as an angel of light" into "sowing thorns and thistles amongst the faithful and even the simple folk."[18] Another eleven statements were considered rash and dangerous but capable of being interpreted in an orthodox manner. His willingness to submit to the Church's authority was reflected in the edict, which stated that Eckhart,

> at the end of his life, professed the Catholic faith, revoked and even condemned the...26 articles, which he admitted having preached [as well as] all other matters written or taught by him, either in the schools or in sermons, that might create in the minds of the faithful an heretical or erroneous impression and one hostile to the true faith.[19]

While the German mystic himself was willing to repudiate his teachings, Meister Eckhart's admirers have not. His unorthodox ideas and speculations have grown in popularity in recent years and have found their most ardent proponent in Matthew Fox. He gives Eckhart the second-highest score on his one-to-five scale of creation-centeredness. More important, Fox has taken Eckhart's condemned teachings and given them his own concrete meanings. Fox quotes Eckhart declaring, "You may call God love; you may call God goodness; but the best name for God is Compassion."[20] Such a statement may not be heretical, depending on the meaning one

---

[18]Raymond B. Blakney, *Meister Eckhart: A Modern Translation* (Harper, 1941) pp xx-xxiv.

[19]James M. Clark, *Meister Eckhart,* pg 258.

[20]Matthew Fox, *A Spirituality Named Compassion*, pg 34.

gives to it. In Father Fox's dictionary, it has the most corrupt meaning possible: *witchcraft*.

The Craft

What is this twisted meaning Fox gives to the word "compassion?" This "compassion" is (supposedly) the source of every virtue. It is the quality that makes us (and Jesus) divine. He calls visualization "extrovert meditation" explaining it as listening to the inner self and uttering "the new images from within outwards. This giving birth to new images is the work of all creative persons."[21]

Compassion is explained in the following excerpt from *A Spirituality Named Compassion*. The word "craft" is a common euphemism for witchcraft. Another is the term "wicca" or "wikke":

> Extrovert meditation, then, gives birth to this new kind of power...a power-with, [which] is properly called compassion. It is a power to imagine with others and to be changed by this imagining. Crafts initiate one into a new kind of power. The German word for power is Kraft. There is no cover-up in this kind of power. "We can't fake craft. It lies in the act.... We do not have the craft or craftmanship, if we do not speak to the light that lives within the earthly materials; this means ALL earthly materials, including men themselves."
>
> [C]ompassion is (the realization of the interconnectedness of all things).[22]

The discussion of the "craft" or witchcraft need not be limited to the traditional image of the medieval wart-nosed hag stirring a bubbling cauldron. Rather, it encompasses most of what would commonly be called paganism. Matthew Fox expands the definition in *Original Blessing:*

---

[21]*Ibid.*, at 134.
[22]*Ibid.*, at 136, 139.

> Native American spirituality is a creation-centered tradi-
> tion, as are the other prepatriarchal religions of the world
> such as African religions, Celtic religion, and the matrifocal
> and Wikke traditions that scholars and practitioners like
> Starhawk are recovering. The contemporary mystical
> movement known as "New Age" can also dialogue and
> create with the creation spiritual tradition.[23]

Miriam Simos (Starhawk) is a practicing witch on the staff of
Matthew Fox's Institute for Culture and Creation Spirituality
(ICCS). Her specialty is the teaching of ritual. Constance Cumbey
calls her, "one of the world's most politically active and important
witches. She is a high priestess in a major coven and has been
[active] politically in both the witches/Neopagan movements as
well as the feminist movement. She is a frequent speaker at New
Age convocations and conferences."[24] Starhawk writes: "In the
Craft, we do not believe in the Goddess—we connect with her;
through the moon, the stars, the ocean, the earth, through trees,
animals, through other human beings, through ourselves. She is
here. She is within us all."[25]

Witchcraft, which is often called "the old religion," is the
worship of (or connection with) "the goddess" or the divine which
it finds in nature. Typical of paganism and the Craft are beliefs in
female deities, the sacredness of nature, power of the individual
will, and the nonexistence of original sin or any division between
good or evil. It is the foundation of feminism.

---

[23]Matthew Fox, *Original Blessing*, pg 16.

[24]Constance Cumbey, *A Planned Deception*, pg 139.

[25]Starhawk, *The Spiral Dance: A Rebirth of the Ancient Religion of
the Great Goddess* (New York, 1979), pg 77f.

Christianity and Feminism

Feminist spirituality has nothing to do with the issues of fair play and equal pay. Those are rights that Christians can support. True feminism is anti-Catholic, anti-Church and anti-Christ.

What the feminists want covers a wide spectrum. Some want absolute identity between the roles of men and women in the church. They support abortion on demand, lesbian rights and in general can be found in the liberal wing politically. These are the moderates. The mainspring groups though, are not looking for a role in the Church—as we know it—at all. They are devoted to the "goddess" who is found in nature and themselves: creation-centered spirituality. Their Wikkan rituals tap the "goddess" power. They would drag God from His heaven and install the mother goddess. While they insist on the goddess, the sexual aspect is secondary to the real appeal—the appeal of having a goddess *which they can control*. She empowers them but makes no demands. She takes no offense at sin, nor calls for any redemption in the traditional sense.

The feminists' dominant mode of operation is to create discontent. They foster frustration, resentment and delusions of persecution by the "unjust patriarchal structures" in the Church, while simultaneously extending the promise of the goddess within. To some the appeal to power and pride is irresistible. The old beliefs lose their grip, and hell signs up another tenant. The point at which one crosses over to the other side comes sooner than most imagine. On the other hand the Church has not been hasty in drawing that line. Consequently, the neo-pagans have a forum for their views. Some of the most public displays occur when feminism's Catholic adherents gather. Such events are invariably blasphemous.

March 9-16, 1985 at Mundelein College in Chicago was the time to celebrate "The Goddess and the Wild Woman." The brochure cover sported a woman, with one breast exposed, dancing and with flowers springing up beneath her feet. Ancient goddesses, Artemis, Athena, Demeter and others stand by. Inside, the brochure speaks of drawing "aside the curtain woven by patriarchal consciousness to reveal within each of us the Goddess and the Wild Woman."[26]

Another gathering of more than 2000 Catholic feminists (as usual, mostly nuns) took place in Washington D.C. on October 10-12, 1986. The conference was entitled "Woman in the Church." Just a sample of the fare:

Speaker, Sister Madonna Kolbenschlag, ripped through "the papacy, the Church, Western civilization, the Judeo-Christian tradition, the Trinity, ("a good ole boy, associating with two other divine males") and monotheism. She asked the participants, in the name of "our elder brother, Jesus," to "be a scandal to the patriarchy." Further,

> Someone once asked me, "What can we salvage from the traditional god-myth that is not destructive?" I don't think that salvaging is any concern of ours. Faith is the process of continually replacing the metaphors for god…. Women today must reclaim their reality from the fantasies, especially through the power of a holistic sexuality, and the right to a free and personally responsible expression of it….[27]

Among the other festivities was a rally in support of Seattle archbishop Raymond Hunthausen as well as the inevitable exhibits by pro-abortion and lesbian groups. There was even a group sponsoring a "feminist liturgy" with a consecration by the women attending. Participants sang and recited poetry and chanted "My name is (X) and I claim my power as church." The priestesses proclaimed, "We are empowered by a loving goddess. We proclaim the power of our foremothers." They spoke of "our exodus from the patriarchal church…." Then at the consecration: "We bless this bread of the eucharist of Woman Church." [28]

---

[26]Frank Morris, *The Wanderer* (April 25,1985) pg 4.

[27]Donna Steichen, *Fidelity* (December, 1986) pg 42.

[28]Joseph Sobran, *The Wanderer* (October 23, 1986) pg 1.

A reporter asked keynote speaker Sister Joan Chittister if the American Church as an institution was ready to stand in opposition to Rome. "Do you want an answer or a prayer?" she replied. "Oh, God, I hope so!"[29]

A feminist philosopher has written of the irreconcilable differences between Christianity and feminism:

> I imagined women functioning as rabbis, priests and ministers...wearing clerical garb and performing clerical duties and suddenly I saw a problem. How could women represent a male god?
>
> God is going to change.... We women are going to bring an end to God...we will be the end of Him. We will change the world so much that He won't fit in any more.
>
> Jesus Christ cannot symbolize the liberation of women.... [F]eminists have to leave Christ and Bible behind them. [30]

This feminist spirituality is probably the most blatant form of heresy in the church today. One wonders how far the leaders of the movement can go without waking up those who, as yet, follow unwittingly. It is not as if the feminists are going around on tiptoe. "Catholic" feminist theologian, Rosemary Ruether writes about her own experience:

> I knew that Ba'al was a real god, the revelation of the mystery of life, the expressions of the depths of being which had broken through into the lives of the people and gave them a key to the mystery of death and rebirth.... As for

---

[29]Steichen, *Fidelity* pg 36.

[30]Naomi R. Goldenberg, *Changing Of The Gods: Feminism and the End of Traditional Religions*, Beacon Press, Boston, 1979, pp 3, 22.

the defects of Ba'al, were they more spectacular than the defects of the biblical God or Messiah, or perhaps less so?

I could hardly tell her [a nun] that my devotion to Mary was somewhat less than my devotion to some far more powerful females that I knew: Isis, Athena, and Artemis![31]

James Hitchcock has pointed out that she held these opinions as an undergraduate, "and thus held them throughout the period when she had a public identity as an orthodox Catholic theologian."[32]

In an April, 1985 interview, Ruether was asked why she even bothered to stay within the Church when so many others with her beliefs had left. Her answer might have come from any one of thousands of modernist Catholics in the Church today: "As a feminist, I can come up with only one reason to stay in the Catholic Church: to try to change it."[33]

The Infection Spreads

American Catholics are not the only ones being exposed to this "tradition." Our brethren to the North are not free of the "Woman Church" phenomenon. The Canadian Bishops have allowed the use of a "Study Kit" on women's issues. The bibliography of this material recommends the reading of radical feminist theologians. One of twelve sessions "contains a liturgy drawn from Wiccan

---

[31]Gregory Baum, ed., *Journeys: The Impact of Personal Experience on Religious Thought*, pp. 43 45.

[32]James Hitchcock, *Catholicism and Modernity: Confrontation or Capitulation?* (Seabury Press, New York, 1979) pg 186.

[33]*U.S. Catholic*, "The editors interview Rosemary Radford Ruether", (April 1985) pg 19.

(witchcraft) sources." One report on the kit maintained that women claimed that the experience had given them a "greater sense of dignity."[34] (Apparently the discovery of your goddess-hood does that for you!)

How far can the return to paganism go? In many places it has gone far. A *National Catholic Reporter* headline reads, "Archbishop summoned for 'witchcraft'."[35] In Germany, there is an officially-registered school for witchcraft. A pharmaceutical company produces tincture of cannabis and other drugs used to enhance pagan rituals.[36] We should take warning from the situation in Brazil, where voodoo cults thrive. On most nights, thousands of followers of the old African religion offer animal sacrifices and while in trances worship spirits which have been merged with the worshippers' favorite Catholic saints. Each cultist is assigned particular spirits, who symbolize Christ, the Virgin Mary and other saints, but are actually demons carried over from the old religion.

The Brazilian church is the largest in the world. Ninety percent of Brazil's 131 million people are Catholic and it is estimated that this mixture of African ritualism and Catholicism is practiced by nearly half of all Brazilian Catholics. The clergy shrug at the problem, admitting that if Rome ordered the pagan practices stopped, no one would listen. One priest said that official church policy opposes the cults "but if we had a hard inflexible attitude we would lose them all."

As American Catholics, we too have slipped far; especially when it is realized that witchcraft or pre-Christian paganism is merely another facet of the New Age movement. Even Father Matthew Fox admits that his Western-oriented creation spirituality is part of the same picture. His Institute for Culture and

---

[34]*The Wanderer*, Canadian Bishops' "Study Kit" (October 23, 1986) pg 1.
[35]*National Catholic Reporter*, September 10, 1982, pg 26.
[36]*America*, November 17, 1984, pg 315.

Creation Spirituality (ICCS) has "become a focus for dialogue with native and Eastern spiritual traditions, the human potential movement, the new physics and the Green Movement."

He says, "Christians and others should not be afraid of terms like 'New Age.' The 'new' can in fact prove to be quite old. For example, a 'new' theology of original blessing is in fact far more ancient than the familiar theology of original sin."

Finally, as if to make certain that no one misses all the connections, the last page of Fox's five point Creation-Centered honor roll reads like a "Who's Who in the New Age movement":

- Teilhard de Chardin
- Carl Jung psychologist, occultist
- Buckminster Fuller, author, *Spaceship Earth*
- Fritjof Capra, author, *The Tao of Physics*
- Starhawk, author, *Dreaming the Dark*
- Marilyn Ferguson, author, *The Aquarian Conspiracy*
- David Spangler, author, *Revelation: Birth of a New Age*

Of course, each author returns the favor and often recommends the others for New Age reading. David Spangler's Lorien Press distributes exclusively New Age titles, some of which were actually dictated by demons. Lorien offers Fox's *Original Blessing*, calling it "a seminal work which Lorien Press is proud to offer."

It is difficult to say how much more popular the New Age movement will become in future years. What is certain is that Christianity is the prime force holding it back. Catholics are the big prize. Unfortunately, the Church, which should be the "salt of the Earth," finds itself in need of salt. If individual Catholics do not act as that salt and stand clearly across the path of this giant, then Matthew Fox's hope may yet come true:

> Beginning with artists in the nineteenth century and extending today to scientists, feminists, New Age mystics, and social prophets, a veritable explosion of creation-centered

spiritual energy is and has been occurring. If entire religious bodies such as Christianity could enter into this expanding spiritual energy field, there is no predicting what powers of passion and compassion might become unleashed.

Father Fox is an insightful man. He sees a need within the Church and moves to fill the vacuum. He points out that we have lost some of the mystery and darkness of the liturgy. The Latin, the smell of many candles and incense, and the somber tones of the Gregorian chant are gone; and gone with these some sense of holiness and awe.

Having noted the need for "darkness" and ritual, Father Fox has a program. He guides us to Native American sweat lodges; to ceremonial dances with drums and fire; and to the witch's Moon Ritual.[37]

While Father Matthew Fox's work continues to grow in popularity in America his teachings have not gone unnoticed in Rome. After a four-year long investigation of his works, Fox's Dominican Order silenced him. Fox announced that the Order had acted "under pressure from the Vatican Congregation of the Doctrine of the Faith, formerly known as the Holy Office of the Inquisition." In Fox's statement to the press on October 20, 1988, he said that it was "an honor to be silenced by the present regime in the Vatican.... [T]he Vatican has grown deaf—deaf to the cries of Mother Earth, deaf to the cries of women, of native peoples and persons of color, of artists...." He spoke of the "need for a spirituality which can heal Mother Earth and usher in an era of a Global Renaissance.... I am proud to be a part of that movement."

Fox's organization, the Friends of Creation Spirituality (FCS), announced that Fox would begin a sabbatical on December 15, 1988 and that he anticipated returning to the Institute for Creation Centered Spirituality in the fall of 1989. FCS also initiated a letter

---

[37]Matthew Fox, *Cosmic Christ*, pp 220-21.

writing campaign to support Fox and the spread of Creation Spirituality. Like his proud modernist forbears, it appears that Father Matthew Fox will carry on the tradition of minimal outward submission coupled with contemptuous defiance.

7.

Close to Home

If your parish hasn't been the scene of New Age stirrings and teachings, it is a real blessing. Some parish priests are completely sold on the New Age movement. Others are obviously influenced by it, perhaps without knowing it. Even then, if the pastor is faithful, even if he is rock solid, he may be undermined by others in a large parish to whom he must turn for assistance. If that were not enough, he may shepherd a fine parish and still see his flock infected. Unless the bishop is equally vigilant, neither is there any guarantee of safety in sending parishioners into diocesan programs.

Sometimes parishioners are only sporadically subjected to New Age references. Maybe Father just read something that he liked and threw it into the homily this week. Last Advent I heard an assistant pastor say, "This is the time of year we remember when a man became God." Now that didn't sound quite right.

On Trinity Sunday we were treated to a sermon on how we need to see God "not just as Father-Son-Spirit, but as Mother-Daughter Spirit," because that is just as legitimate a viewpoint as the male God perspective. A week later we were given Part Two on "seeing God as mother." There is certainly nothing wrong with saying that God has what have traditionally been thought of as feminine qualities, such as nurturing. How else to explain Jesus's lament over Jerusalem: "How often would I have gathered thy children together, as a hen gathers her young under her wings, but thou wouldst not!" (Matthew 23:37). But then, God has chosen to reveal himself as Father. It is as if He were telling us that while He is not a man, we can best relate to him as "Father."

The feminists will argue that the God/Goddess revealed herself/himself as a male (Father and Son) because it was a prerequisite in the culture of the period. That much said, they then prove exactly the opposite in their tirade against the patriarchal systems of the Judeo/Christian religion. They point out that there was a time (before Abraham's God appeared) when religion was matriarchal. Even throughout the history of the Old Testament the Israelite's neighbors worshipped both male and female gods. Logically then, if the idea of a female deity was common, why should God have had any practical need to conform to patriarchal customs? The best explanation is the simplest. He revealed Himself in exactly the way in which He desired to be known. It is our duty as His creatures to accept it.

Catholics of Orange, California were recently treated to a Buddhist healing service at the Spirituality Center for the Sisters of St. Joseph of Orange. Five Tibetan monks chanted mantras and rang bells. Wearing headdresses topped with skulls, the monks danced, banged a drum and tooted a horn. At intermission, Buddhist and New Age materials were offered for sale.

"As a Christian, I'm afraid to read this," said one Catholic woman.

"With all bad things, there's some good," replied the reassuring Sister as she collected the cash.

A brief talk on Buddhism followed and then the pagan ritual concluded with a dance for which the monks put on a horse costume.[1]

---

[1] *The Wanderer*, November 23, 1989, pg 8.

For two weeks straight the Sunday bulletin trumpeted the upcoming speaking engagement of Rosemary Ruether at the University of Missouri campus Newman Center on April 29, 1988. The rainbow backdrop to the altar was appropriate for the occasion as this professor of theology railed against the unjust patriarchal structures of the Church. Describing her own spirituality as a "creation-based spirituality" (remember Matthew Fox?), she explained her resistance to "spiritualities which make other worldly splits."

This is pantheism. It rejects the distinction between nature and spirit which Scripture clearly reveals and the Church teaches. Speaking of redemption and Jesus (who "got himself strung up"), she said, "Nobody can save the world by himself. The only way you can save the whole world is by all of us together." A few of Ruether's listeners shifted uneasily in their seats, but most were in accord. Could she—even as she stood at the altar in front of the crucified Christ—could she have forgotten that "For since by a man came death, by a man also comes resurrection of the dead. For as in Adam all die, so in Christ all will be made to live" (1 Corinthians 15:21).[2] Naturally, we must co-operate in this salvation, but the individual will stand or fall on his own faith and corresponding works. Whether together or separately, we humans will never save the world.

This is a great lie of the New Age movement and shows a striking similarity to a supposedly non-religious belief—that of secular humanism. The *Humanist Manifesto II* declares: "[H]umans are responsible for what we are or will become. No deity will save us; we must save ourselves." The apparent difference between the

---

[2]Actually the feminists studiously avoid this verse, because it undermines their favorite myth: that the Church persecutes women because *they* are responsible for original sin. Without this and other paranoid accusations they would be much less effective in getting their listeners lathered up for a fight (in fact the formation of a Womanchurch group was the objective for this particular get-together.

mystical New Age view and the naturalist/agnostic view is no real difference at all. Both viewpoints are in perfect agreement in believing that nature is everything. Each exalts both human potential and scientific progress. Each makes man a god, answerable only to himself. One is hard pressed to draw dividing lines that differentiate other than by degree.

Sometimes Catholic New Agers will form parachurch organizations, open to all faiths, and thus not specifically "Catholic," but with a strong Catholic membership, Catholic outreach and support in the Catholic community. In Kansas City, Missouri Woman-Source is such an organization. WomanSource president Carol Meyer is an ex-nun who "saw a need for more support in the community for the empowerment of women." She is also the former associate director of the editorial department of Credence Cassettes, a division of the National Catholic Reporter publishing company and a leading "Catholic" purveyor of New Age tapes. She and eleven other women, including another nun (a Sister of Charity), started the group in October 1986. Funded by dues, donations and grants, they received their first grant, $1000, from the Sisters of Loretto.

WomanSource operates a "drop-in center" which includes a meditation room. A friend who has visited the center described a "stark room with a round rug on the floor. On the rug was a small clay pot for a candle. Also on the rug was a statue of a woman, and behind the statue, leaning against the wall, was a very large framed picture of Stonehenge." My friend wondered what God they prayed to in that room. Her guide said, "I am a Catholic, but anyone can pray to whoever they feel like or want to."

The April/May, 1988 issue of the WomanSource newsletter promoted a "self-awareness group" which was scheduled to meet for six consecutive Saturdays and would—among other things—explore "matriarchal societies' histories and *how to use the goddess' energy for personal empowerment*." Even if such paganism received no actual support from the Church it would still be worth warning Catholic women about what they are getting into. But the Kansas City diocese does not merely acquiesce in the matter, but is actually a warm home for WomanSource. Consider how likely local Catholics are to take warning when even the official diocesan paper has run a positive article on WomanSource and has carried WomanSource events in the weekly calendar. The same goes when local Catholic churches open their facilities to the group.

On February 26, 1988 WomanSource offered a retreat at the Franciscan Prayer Center in Independence, Missouri. Called "The Healing Art of Meditation," the experience was to include "Tibetan Buddhism, Visualization, Centering, Chakra Balancing, Sufi Blessing, *Tai-Chi* and Clay Meditation."

Another group, Woman Alive, presented a program called WomanSpirit Rising (funny how these New Age feminists always run the word "woman" and something else together). This New Age event was held at the Maria Center of the School Sisters of Notre Dame in St Louis, Missouri, over Halloween weekend, 1987. Jolene Unnerstall, co-ordinator for Woman Alive and ex-Sister of Notre Dame, was joined by fellow Aquarians in presenting workshops involving pure pagan occultism. A few of their "Out on a Limb" style topics:

THE GODDESS WITHIN
Recognition of the archetypal patterns of ancient Goddesses inspires us to appreciate the power and presence of divine qualities within ourselves and to enjoy recognizing the unique beauty of the goddesses in our friends and family.

PAST LIVES and PRESENT WISDOM
Jolene has served as a reader of Akashic records as well as led hundreds of seekers to explore their own past-life memories. We will explore the purpose and value of uncovering past life wisdom and applying it to today's experience.

CHAKRAS: Spiritual Energy Centers

The "chakra" system of understanding our spiritual energy is a tool for wholesomeness. We will experience a meditation for chakra balancing....

CHANNELING YOUR HIGH SELF

Explore the techniques and processes of channeling and how to use channeled information to enhance spiritual understanding. Group channeling will be the highlight of the session. Participants can plan to get some questions of a spiritual nature answered through the channeling process.

CRYSTALS for MEDITATION

Crystals can be used as a tool for amplifying consciousness and as such can be an aid to focusing in meditation and healing. Presents how to select and use crystals wisely.

How can it be that any Catholic would be involved with such unmixed spiritual venom? Because they believe that no Catholic institution would permit their facilities to be used for such things as the calling up of demons for the purpose of giving advice. Maybe one should not assume anything anymore.

One of the most remarkable New Age successes has to be the breeziness with which New Age meditation is recommended— even in the Church—for any Catholic who is interested. I read this notice in our parish bulletin and decided to check it out for myself:

CENTERING PRAYER: Fr. Bob will make a presentation on "Centering Prayer," a method of meditation on Monday, March 2, at 7:45pm in Classroom 2 in the parish hall. All are invited.

Our assistant pastor began speaking to our group, which was made up of eight or ten women plus myself. He introduced the topic explaining that in 1976, Pope Paul VI asked a leader of the Cistercian order to share his order's prayer methods with other religious communities. A decade later, the Pope's request now serves as the reason that our self-appointed little group was about to be taught Hindu meditation. He began:

"The purpose of the technique is to move our minds to a different state of consciousness" he told us. "The idea is that the experience should sustain us during the time we are not meditating. We go to a deeper level, searching for God or Jesus whom we believe to be there. This is accomplished through the use of the *Love Word* [mantra] which is repeated just often enough to keep you centered. Some people feel it helps to tie the Love Word into their breathing. You'll notice how it slows as you go deeper."

"At that level," he concluded, "you feel God. Faith is no longer necessary."

At this point, we moved into the church building to have a go at it ourselves. We sat in the dark pews for 25 minutes. I spent the first ten minutes emptying my brain in hopes that God would start talking or moving or whatever.

"How would I know it was Him?" I had wondered....

"This is ridiculous!" I thought, as I abandoned the effort and instead used the remaining time to initiate a more conventional and effective prayer. Finally, Father spoke, bringing us back to our normal waking level of consciousness and dismissing us with his hope that meditation would become a frequent and profitable experience. It seemed a frivolous ending for what might for some turn out to be very deep water.

I expressed my concern to one friend, who although favorably disposed to such meditation from his seminary experience, was disturbed at the dangers of its indiscriminate spread and these unguided pilgrimages into the unknown. Another priest friend listened to my concerns about the New Age meditation and the Church and just shrugged. "We have much to learn from the Hindus," he told me.

The New Age on Tape

What can a Catholic New Ager do to accelerate his downward slide if he has no New Age center in his town and if his pastor won't let the poison in the church door? He can find plenty of New Age books and tapes and he won't have to step outside "Catholic" sources to do it. Such Catholic suppliers as Credence Cassettes (a service of the National Catholic Reporter Publishing Co.) and Paulist Press promote the rubbish. Even Orbis Books (Maryknoll Fathers) has given the New Age some catalog space—while still carrying the full line of their trademark "liberation theology" titles. A few of the topics/authors available from Credence Cassettes:

- Mantra Chanting; the "Groaning Prayer Cassette"
- A Jesuit theologian who has traveled in Asia and studied Eastern prayer teaches Hatha Yoga.
- Guided Meditations/Imagery
- Lots of New Age (healing) music
- The seven petitions of the LORD'S Prayer are correlated with the seven occult energy centers from the East (*chakras*). The speaker explains how these petitions and chakras describe various postures. With New Age music accompaniment.
- Dream Interpretation and the occultist psychologist C.G. Jung
- Ed Hays, Bede Griffiths, Thomas Merton,
- Ira Progoff journaling; The Spirituality of Teilhard de Chardin
- WOMANCHURCH / Rosemary Ruether

How ironic that this same catalog (Spring/Summer 1988) has a cassette entitled "Traditional Catholic Hymns" marked down to half price.

Silva Mind Control

It would be difficult to find a system of practice more destructive of Christian faith than the Silva Mind Control Method. More difficult yet is to imagine it being promoted and taught in a Catholic Church. The system features both the meditative state of eastern religion and the pagan visualization techniques which give the method its power. In the Silva Method, the student first learns to achieve an altered state of consciousness ("counting down to your level"). Through a series of meditations one learns relaxation and problem solving.

The student begins to utilize visualization by creating a "Mental Screen" within the imagination. The student projects onto the screen whatever image he wishes to concentrate upon. The meditations purport to ease pain, speed learning and break bad habits. These though, are just the baby steps of this method.

On the third day of training, students learn to project themselves, through their imaginations, into buildings, walls, metal objects and even inside the body of a pet (in preparation for projections into human bodies). Finally the student is ready to construct his laboratory. In deep meditation, the mind control student creates a refuge of his choosing. A cozy library, a submarine, a cave or whatever he likes. It is furnished with desk and chair, filing cabinets, clock and calendar. Additionally, the student adds various tools: healing salves, chemicals, a stereo playing soothing music.

In the laboratory, the meditating student summons two "counselors," male and female. These "counselors" are to be consulted in full confidence. Their guidance supposedly confers great power (for good only, of course). Upon their appearance in the laboratory, they may or may not turn out to be the persons the student had hoped for. Who are these "counselors" Mr. Silva provides? In *The Silva Mind Control Method*, he answers:

> We are not sure—perhaps some figment of our archetypal imagination, perhaps an embodiment of the inner voice, perhaps something more. What we do know is that, once

we meet our counselors and learn to work with them, the association is respectful and priceless.[3]

In her book, *The Beautiful Side of Evil*, Johanna Michaelsen tells of her experience with the Silva Method. She chose Jesus and Sarah Bernhardt (Johanna was interested in acting) as her counselors. At the Mind Control class, she went to her level and entered her laboratory where her counselors, Jesus and Sarah revealed themselves to her. She fell at Jesus' feet. Before dismissing the class, the instructor admonished the students not to try to call up their counselors that evening at home. That night, ignoring the warning, she counted down to her level and as she sat in the blue velvet armchair in her laboratory facing the door:

> "Oh Lord," I prayed, "please, reveal the counselors I'm truly meant to have." The chamber door began lowering— the same radiance shining from behind it—but something was wrong.... The hair was wild and matted, the forehead was covered with coarse fur and the eyes were slanted, gleaming and wild.... Fresh blood smeared the muzzle and oozed down long white fangs.... Yet the rest of the figure was the same as before, covered in a long linen robe and gleaming.[4]

The next day at mind control class—discounting the experience the night before—she learned to accept the werewolf faces of Jesus and Sarah. That day she learned to psychically diagnose the illnesses of people far away whom she had never met.

Later, she became the assistant to a psychic surgeon whose body was possessed by a spirit being who performed surgery with

---

[3]José Silva, Phillip Miele, *The Silva Mind Control Method* (Simon and Schuster, New York, 1977) pg 87.

[4]Johanna Michaelsen, *The Beautiful Side of Evil* (Harvest House, Eugene, Oregon, 1982) pg 75.

unsterilized knives and scissors and without anesthetic.[5] Her story is worth reading for anyone who doubts that evil can appear as beautiful as anyone can imagine.

As with other meditation systems, Silva Mind Control is supposed to be absolutely harmless. Jose Silva claims that it is impossible to do evil while at your meditative level.[6] On the other hand, the spirit being who controlled the psychic surgeon informed Johanna that "a person who wishes another one evil strongly enough can cause dark beings to focus upon him."[7] It has to make one wonder why openly occult sources seem willing to admit to the dangers of esoteric meditation but the supposed "self-improvement" types and "Christian" supporters of the techniques fall all over themselves in denying the dangers.

What has this to do with Roman Catholics? We're signing up at $325 apiece (the cost of the Silva course) to learn to control these powers. I am reminded of St. Peter's reaction to Simon the magician who was so impressed with the Apostles' power that he attempted to buy it. Peter replied, "Thy money go to destruction with thee, because thou hast thought that the gift of God could be purchased with money." (Acts 8:19-20).

Most recently I ran into literature from a group in Indianapolis called "The Hermitage." While "The Hermitage" calls itself an ecumenical organization, its founding director is a Catholic priest who teaches the Silva Method as well as other meditation courses. The Hermitage offers courses in The Silva Method of Mind Development, Silva Method for Children (done with puppets), Christian Astrology & Buddhist meditation. Their newsletter attracts advertisers offering occult books and yoga therapy, numerology services, shamanism, private healings and the like. While this outfit is not an overtly Catholic enterprise, Catholic organizations

---

[5] *Ibid.* at 77, 85.
[6] Jose Silva, *Silva Mind Control*, at 35.
[7] Michaelsen, *Beautiful Side of Evil*, at 133.

seem to be open to it. I called a Catholic parish in Omaha that was offering the Hermitage's Silva Method that same week. The secretary verified the ongoing (4 day) course. I asked if some people didn't object to having this course in the church. "Oh no," she told me, "Father [the pastor] has had these here in prior years."

I spoke with the Omaha co-ordinator for the Hermitage (also a Catholic). She said the best thing about the course was the realization of being "at one with others and with the universe." I asked, "Do you see any similarity between Silva meditation and what is now called Centering Prayer?"

"It's all *exactly* the same thing!" she insisted. "All of these things (meditation techniques) are the same thing." She invited me to the course on "Successful Living"—achieving success through meditation—which was scheduled for the coming weekend. I passed up the opportunity, figuring that if I needed that sort of thing I could find it a lot closer to home. For it is not in Omaha alone that someone seems to be asleep at the wheel. I noticed from their schedule that the next stop on the Hermitage's Silva Method road show was to be a convent in Cleveland.

8.

Fight It? . . . or Forget It?

I hope someone would criticize a book like this. I hope they would ask why it should even be written. Why drag up all this ugly material and cite the involvement of members of our own Church? My answer would be to agree. After all, we have the Church to show us the truth. We have the Bible, God's Word, to shine its light through the mess.

Ideally, our church leaders will be faithful, but some are not. The strengths of the Catholic Church—our traditions and hierarchy—are no strengths unless the shepherds are faithful at every level. Many Catholics, regrettably, have allowed their trust in the hierarchy to deaden their capacity to think for themselves. When the sermon leaves you scratching your head, don't immediately question your Catholic education or your intelligence. The most common reaction of people exposed to New Age ideas from the pulpit is to assume there must be something faulty in themselves whenever ideas don't strike a pleasing chord. One need not be a theologian to realize that the homily is rotten when the subject is the "Mother Goddess."

It is the greatest irony that the very Catholics who seek to serve God and hunger most for Him are the most endangered. Having no reason to mistrust their seminary professor, local pastor or diocesan officials, they hand their spiritual development over to those who would destroy them. They get involved in C.C.D.

programs or become communion ministers or lectors. Typically, and reasonably, they are expected to take a series of courses to prepare them for these responsibilities. They take retreats or other weekend programs for their spiritual growth. Too often though, they are taught to devalue the Scripture, to discount the miracles and divinity of Christ and to bare their minds to the spiritual dynamite of Eastern meditation. If they refuse to believe the lies of the "new spirituality," they can look forward to being ridiculed by eloquent, educated teachers.

Ideally, Catholics will study the Bible for themselves imitating the Bereans of the New Testament who "studied the scriptures to see whether these things were so" (Acts 17:11). But we have not. Sadly, our most effective barriers to error have come down.

It should be clear that many unwary and innocent Catholics are being pulled in. Catholic clergy and laity are joining the New Age at least as eagerly as the rest of the world. A Jesuit professor of philosophy confesses to be a believer in astrology. One Catholic astrologer who has had many priests come to her for advice has said: "Now a lot of Catholics in my congregation come to me either as students or clients. The clergy have never given me a problem; only Catholics who consider it superstitious and fundamentalists who interpret the Bible very literally and often incorrectly."[1]

A Catholic theologian has written a book attempting to reconcile Christian belief with psychic phenomena. He calls Jesus a "human being...blessed and gifted with incredible paranormal and psychokinetic powers."[2]

On another front, Catholic publishers have been eager to produce New Age books and other materials. Whether they know what they do or are simply following the crowd, who can say? But what is not doubtful is the unmistakable fact of the shift. I have

[1]*Our Sunday Visitor*, January 26, 1986, pg 8.

[2]John J. Heaney, *The Sacred and the Psychic: Parapsychology & Christian Theology* (Paulist Press, New York, 1984) pg 43.

watched the cassette catalog published by the *National Catholic Reporter* (see chapter seven) grow more and more New Age with each issue. Its offerings now include much material formerly found only in occult book stores.

Also, we must remain watchful outside the church doors as well. Not everyone is making their entrance into the New Age movement through spiritual pathways. Many enter in through various other modes of social transformation. True, the New Age movement is first a spiritual movement, but additionally, it is a totalitarian movement encompassing all aspects of life including politics and economics. In the business community, the New Age concept of visualization is the basis of success tapes and seminars. In the schools, it surfaces as global education, emphasizing social values and "planetary consciousness" while downplaying reading, math and national independence.

Darkness Ahead?

Often the "new ideas" are appealing. Not all New Age solutions are bad—at least not at first glance. Still, other New Age goals are quite hopeless but people, nonetheless, are willing to grasp for them in desperation.

Some time ago, a television movie called *The Day After* aired. Its portrayal of the aftermath of nuclear war was particularly dismaying and ominous. The next day, I was discussing the program with a friend who was more than a little discouraged by it. He volunteered his solution to the problem of nuclear war:

"I've figured out that there is only one way out of this."

I smiled and said "Really?" I thought a joke was coming.

"Well sure," he said, "the only permanent solution is to have a single world government!" He was brightening now as the thought solidified in his mind, obviously delighted with himself.

"It will never work," I told him.

"Why not?" he asked as his solution developed a crack. "You'd have to kill too many people," I continued, "Me for one; I'd never go along and I'm sure plenty of others would not either."

He glared at me and for a moment I sensed his anger; even a flash of hatred. It made me strangely uncomfortable. I wasn't surprised that normally level-headed people would seize upon radical ideas. What was surprising was the grip that those ideas have on them; and the disdain that falls on others not similarly transformed. One wonders what the New Agers would do with the Christians if they ever obtained political power. Their writings speak of "cleansings" and removing us from the physical plane. They speak of reducing the population by a billion or two, or three; and of a new natural selection which involves destruction to clear the way for evolutionary progress.

"The Wild Truth"

Books promoting the New Age movement often display a special pride in enumerating the dozens of entrance-ways into the movement. In *The Aquarian Conspiracy*, Marilyn Ferguson wrote of "trigger" experiences that focus awareness on awareness. Among the triggers are biofeedback, music meditation, hypnosis, self-hypnosis, seminars like *est* or Silva Mind Control, primal therapy, gestalt therapy, and the martial arts. She also reported the disciplines below as being instrumental in personal change:

- Zen Buddhism
- Yoga
- "Christian" mysticism
- Journals and dream journals
- Psychosynthesis
- Jungian therapy
- Transcendental Meditation
- Tibetan Buddhism

- Sufism
- Transactional analysis[3]

It would seem that the ways into the New Age are as wide and varied as the individuals who enter it. The way is easy and contrasts sharply with the truth that Jesus gave us:

> Enter through the narrow gate. For wide is the gate and broad is the way that leads to destruction, and many there are who enter that way. How narrow the gate and close the way that leads to life! And few there are who find it! (Matthew 7:13,14)

G.K. Chesterton wrote about the need for orthodoxy. To him the narrow way was not restrictive, but glorious:

> Last and most important, it is exactly this which explains what is so inexplicable to all the modern critics of the history of Christianity. I mean the monstrous wars about small points of theology, the earthquakes of emotion about a gesture or a word. It was only a matter of an inch; but an inch is everything when you are balancing.
>
> Doctrines had to be defined within strict limits, even in order that man might enjoy general human liberties. The Church had to be careful, only if the world might be careless.
>
> This is the thrilling romance of Orthodoxy. People have fallen into the foolish habit of speaking of orthodoxy as something heavy, humdrum and safe. There never was anything so perilous or so exciting as orthodoxy. It was sanity: and to be sane is more dramatic than to be mad. It was the equilibrium of a man behind madly rushing horses.
>
> It is easy to be a madman: It is easy to be a heretic. It is always easy to let the age have its head; the difficult thing is to keep one's own. It is always easy to be a modernist; as it is easy to be a snob. To have fallen into any of those open

---

[3]Marilyn Ferguson, *The Aquarian Conspiracy*, pp 85-87.

traps of error and exaggeration which fashion after fashion and sect after sect set along the historic path of Christendom—that would indeed have been simple. It is always simple to fall; there are an infinity of angles at which one falls, only one at which one stands. To have fallen into any one of the fads from Gnosticism to Christian Science would indeed have been obvious and tame. But to have avoided them all has been one whirling adventure, and in my vision the heavenly chariot flies thundering through the ages; the dull heresies sprawling and prostrate, the wild truth reeling but erect.[4]

The Final Confrontation?

In a 1976 visit to the United States, Pope John Paul II (then Karol Cardinal Wojtyla) spoke prophetically of a final crisis coming upon the Church:

> We are now standing in the face of the greatest historical confrontation humanity has gone through. I do not think that wide circles of the American society or wide circles of the Christian community realize this fully. We are now facing the final confrontation between the Church and the anti-Church, of the Gospel versus the anti-Gospel. This confrontation lies within the plans of divine Providence; it is a trial which the whole Church... must take up.[5]

The "confrontation" is assuming an increasingly solid shape, but we still haven't a complete picture. What we must not do when looking at the New Age movement is to see just so many separate heresies. The term networking was first embraced by New Agers, but has now come into general usage. A useful concept, networking is a method of linking people together in the manner of a fish net.

---

[4]G.K. Chesterton, *Orthodoxy* (Image Books, Garden City, New York, N.Y., 1959) pp 100-101.

[5]*Wall Street Journal*, November 9, 1978, originally quoted in the *New York City News.*

The non-hierarchical structure of the network with its "knots" or nodes makes it appear headless and less potent than it is. But just as the fish that gets caught in the net knows, it works very well. These manifestations of the New Age movement in the Church are truly the tentacles of the same adversary, just as St. Pius X cautioned: "[T]he Modernists...present their doctrines without order and systematic arrangement into one whole, scattered and disjointed one from another, so as to appear to be in doubt and uncertainty, while they are in reality firm and steadfast...."[6]

It might even be called a conspiracy, but not in the conventional sense. Most New Agers themselves don't have *the plan* in front of them as they work. Instead, the collusion is one of mutual goals, shared values, and a common spiritual orientation. The reader should not misunderstand. There is a *real* conspiracy and it is orchestrated from a single source: the Devil of Hell. The fight is about nothing else. It is about standing firm and faithful. It is taking the trouble to question new ideas (however popular) to see if they square with the truth.

We must question seemingly supernatural events. The forces of evil are quite capable of producing signs and wonders. Why are people so eager to chase after such things? We are Christians. We believe in miracles and we know that Satan is able to counterfeit them also. With this in mind, remember it is the message that counts. We have been warned:

> Beloved, do not believe every spirit, but test the spirits to see whether they are of God; because many false prophets have gone forth into the world. By this is the spirit of God known: every spirit that confesses that Jesus Christ has come in the flesh, is of God. And every spirit that severs Jesus, is not of God, but is of Anti-christ.... (I John 4:1-3)

---

[6]Pius X, *Pascendi* at 6.

"Every spirit which severs Jesus" refers to the separation of Jesus from the "office" of the Christ. This is precisely what the New Agers and the world religion advocates have done with Jesus. Apparent miracles and religious feelings aside, if the message is wrong, then *it is not of God*. Our vigilance should be commensurate with the fury and hatred of our enemy. Surely, the New Age movement is the hottest trick in his bag.

This book might have been much longer except that it has not been my purpose to fill in all the blanks, exposing the complete scope of the "conspiracy." It is not for everyone to make a long study of it, but rather to be aware; and to be ready to resist when necessary. Don't doubt for a moment that lay people are capable of fighting back.

Once, as a CCD teacher, I was required to attend certain ongoing courses sponsored by the diocese in order to remain a certified teacher. Having been exposed to Matthew Fox's ideas and "encounter group" type exercises in earlier classes, I hoped the upcoming class on the scriptures would be a welcome change. Held on two consecutive Saturdays, this course was simply an eight hour attack on the Bible. The first Saturday, the instructor tore apart the Old Testament, stripping it of all historic and prophetic value. A week later, he taught us that the miracles recorded in the New Testament never really happened! He allowed only the resurrection. (I suppose he wasn't ready to take that one on!)

In light of the trash we had already been subjected to, I decided I'd had enough and raised my hand. He stopped and I said: "I have always been taught that the Gospel stories are true and that they support the truth of Christianity. Now it is very nice spring day out and if all of this is just a fairy story then we are wasting our time. We ought to go home and do more important things."

I sat back down, feeling more than half like an idiot. The teacher stared for a moment, somehow torn between anger and pity for this ignorant wretch. Just as he was about to open his mouth to crush me someone else spoke up: "He's right. I believe the same thing."

"Yeah, me too," said another, and another until all 25 of us had come down in perfect opposition to his propaganda. Did he argue with us? No; he sensed he was beaten and worked quickly to fall into line, backpeddling faster than a politician. I almost think he liked it.

The point is that we lay people are not powerless. In many cases we have freedom to act where the clergy cannot. If a faithful priest or nun raises a complaint she may be told to "stay out of it." How many of them are in a position to resist such orders to keep their mouths closed and their heads down. They need our support and prayers. The laity, on the other hand, are less easily restrained. Still, our opposition may be costly. That was the lesson learned by the parishioners at St. Boniface in Stewart, Minnesota. Operating without a resident pastor, the church was assigned a nun as "parish minister." Unfortunately, she was a Matthew Fox devotée who replaced orthodox teachings with worship of self and nature.

Her Saturday "eucharists" (with pre-consecrated hosts but no priest) for CCD teachers were especially disturbing. A polyester globe (the "Hugg-A-Planet" pillow) replaced the crucifix. There were prayers to "Our Mother" and prayer intentions for "men and boys deluded by false notions of manhood." It was only a matter of time before parishioners were fed up and took the matter to the bishop.

The bishop's response was decisive: Nearly all the parishioners must either submit to a year of group psychotherapy (at their own expense) or the parish would be virtually shut down. Since too few church members were willing to turn themselves over to the straighteners, all Masses, the Sacraments and other organized church functions were forbidden. The bishop's only criticism of the New Age nun was that she went "too fast."[7] No, it was the orthodox members of St. Boniface Catholic Church that needed help. One might ask whether the faithful should have acquiesced in the pagan

---

[7]Donna Steichen, *Fidelity* (September 1989) pg 28.

activities of their sister rather than lose the Church in their community. But we must remember why we come to the Church. We come for spiritual reasons and have very little to lose once the Church has failed in its spiritual purpose.

The struggle is difficult. It is more likely than not that your pastor is open to New Age ideas. Matthew Fox is quoted from the pulpit. Too many bishops are more worried over feminist concerns than they are about the loss of the faith. Even Catholics with no interest in New Age practices are becoming accustomed to its concepts; they should be well primed by the time Creation-Centered Spirituality becomes the norm in our churches. But our resistance is neither hopeless nor futile.

The situation reminds me of a case that was recently decided by the Missouri Supreme Court. Over the past few years the courts in one state after another have ruled that human beings could be starved to death when they were found to have an inadequate "quality of life." By the fall of 1988, 16 states had found one legal theory or another by which they might kill a person who was permanently unconscious—or nearly so—even though not terminally ill. The euthanasia proponents had won a long series of victories, until the courageous judges of this one court broke the string and said no. They said that they did not care what every other state had said—every other state is wrong! Now it remains to be seen what happens next,[8] but at least the next judge—the next court—will have another opinion to consider. Because four men had the fortitude to stand when it would have been so much easier to fall.

Our situation is much the same. While we cannot draw the lines for an entire state we can let others know where we stand. Realistically, it is your brother in the next pew who is most apt to be open to reason. Not having the benefit of a modernist seminary educa-

---

[8]By the time this book is in print, the U.S. Supreme Court will have heard (and probably decided) the *Cruzan* case.

tion he could rely more on common sense and his or her Catholic upbringing. That is the strongest card to play. Nobody remembers God the Mother from grade school. Nobody used to be taught to visualize demons masquerading as Jesus. Nobody used to minimize the fact of original sin so as to better celebrate our "Original Blessing."

We must have thicker skins. We must stand, even as others fall around us. If the latest ideas reek of pantheism, the problem is not with our noses. There is nothing wrong with the gospel that we first learned. Yes, we are often sinful. And unjust. And unkind. But let us not be driven into the inhuman arms of the New Age by the seeming hopelessness of this age. Salvation lies not in the New Age, but where it always has and always will endure: In the merits of Jesus Christ our Lord.

Appendix.

New Age Politics, Economics and Social Change

A Partial Agenda

A weakening of the national government by two means:

- political decentralization, with power held by regional and local governments.
- transfer of sovereign national power to a global authority. Many plans for this exist. One is the Constitution for the Federation of the Earth. It provides for a tri-lateral parliament made up of an elected or appointed House of Nations, an elected House of Peoples and a nominated House of Counselors from the world's universities. Also, there would be a world judiciary, a world executive, and of course, a world police force.

Regular transfer payments from industrial to developing countries:

- third world debt would be converted to outright grants. Aid would be withheld from countries resisting New Age reform.

Sustainable economics:

- only renewable resources would be developed. Nations and/or Corporations which use non-renewable resources would pay a severance royalty to compensate for their irresponsibility.
- the automobile would become uncommon. People would move to smaller communities. Twenty percent of us would return to the farm. Mass transit would serve those who remained in cities.

Appropriate Technology (A.T.), also known as human scale, intermediate or alternate technology:

- A.T. is small, cheap, simple, ecologically benign and sensitive to natural harmonies. It shows a preference for decentralization and nonmaterial values. It is spiritual. Windmills are A.T. Bulldozers are not.

Minimum/Maximum Incomes:

- everyone would be guaranteed a minimum income. This would free up people who want to develop themselves outside traditional jobs. The income tax would provide for total confiscation of earnings above a certain level. Money should not be a problem because every one would live under "voluntary simplicity."

Population control:

- it would be necessary to reduce the present world—and U.S.—population by 30% or more. Abortion would remain freely available and tax laws would penalize families with more than their share of children.

Repeal of all compulsory education laws:
- Values education would take priority over basic literacy and math.

Extension of rights to children:
- the rights, duties, and responsibilities of adults would be given to children at much earlier age levels. They would choose to live where and how they wished. Whether to be educated or not; to make contracts, collect welfare and engage in sex acts with any partner(s) of their choosing.

Elimination of Crime:
- crime would immediately be cut in half by repealing half of the criminal laws. All drugs, gambling, prostitution and sexual perversions would be legal.
- nearly all prisons would be closed, in favor of rehabilitation hostels.

Proper Use of the Media:
- The "fairness doctrine" would be enforced. Authorities would oversee the press to insure against one-sided reporting.
- Advertising of food not deemed healthful would not be permitted.

Abolition of any licensing of health practitioners.
- M.D.'s would be no more legitimate than psychic healers, witch doctors, hypnotists, Indian medicine men, vitamin peddlers and acupuncturists.

Suggested Reading

Note: Some of the authors listed below are Protestant writers. They are offered not for their agreement with Catholic teaching, but for their helpfulness in illuminating the New Age movement.

A Catechism of Modernism, by Rev. J. B. Lemius, O.M.I

Hidden Dangers of the Rainbow, by Constance Cumbey

A Planned Deception, by Constance Cumbey

A Crisis of Truth, by Ralph Martin

The Seduction of Christianity, by Dave Hunt

Beyond Seduction, by Dave Hunt

Teilhardism and the New Religion, by Wolfgang Smith

The AntiChrist, by Vincent Miceli

The Twisted Cross, by Joseph Carr

Gods of the New Age, by Caryl Matrisciana

Rest from the Quest, by Ellisa Lindsey McClain

The Beautiful Side of Evil, by Johanna Michaelson

Partisans of Error, by Michael Davies

Globalism: America's Demise, by William M. Bowen, Jr.

Original Sin in the Light of Modern Science, by Rev. Patrick O'Connell

Index